MW00675184

CAVEMEN IN BABYLAND

What New and Expecting Mommies

Should Know about New Daddies

(So That They Won't Kill Them)

by

Kindred Howard

Rameses Publishing

Powder Springs, Georgia

www.cavemeninbabyland.com

Rameses Publishing
Powder Springs, Georgia

Copyright © 2011 by Kindred Howard

Cover design by KB Howard and New Life Image
Book design by Zuzana Urbanek, www.z-ink.net

All rights reserved.

No part of this book may be reproduced in any form or by any electronic or mechanical means including information storage and retrieval systems, without permission in writing from the author. The only exception is by a reviewer, who may quote short excerpts in a review.

Printed in the United States of America

First Printing: July 2011

Howard, Kindred
        Cavemen in Babyland: What New and Expecting Mommies Should
        Know about New Daddies (So That They Won't Kill Them)

ISBN-10 098363310X
ISBN-13 9780983633105

A Caveman Dedication

This book is dedicated to my best friend and wife of fourteen years, Meredith. When we first met in 1996, I immediately thought she had the most beautiful smile I had ever seen. I still do. After fourteen years, Meredith is still the love of my life and the woman I want to spend the rest of my life with. *Cavemen in Babyland* would not have been written without her. She is and forever will be my inspiration, and I am deeply grateful and humbled to know that she has chosen to be my biggest fan. Thanks, Mere. I love you.

Caveman
Acknowledgements

The completion of this book would not have been possible without the love, support, and efforts of many key people. First and foremost, I want to thank my beautiful wife, Meredith, who has always believed in me and encouraged me to pursue my dreams and passions. It is greatly because of her faith, vision, unending encouragement, and (when needed) great patience that I have had the opportunity and fortitude to embark upon and complete this project. Secondly, I must thank my wonderful children Emerson, William, Carson, Samuel, and Asher. They are truly the joy of their parents' lives, and it is because of them that writing this book has been a labor of love (not to mention all the material with which they have provided me).

I also want to thank John Rosemond who has become a good friend and mentor to me as I strive to help others as a professional parent coach. Although we have known each other only a short while, John has already had a profound impact on my life and my parenting. Additionally, I owe a debt of gratitude to my former colleagues and mentors in the ministry—Rick Maule,

Ron Drabot, and Ross Mackenzie—for the great examples they set as husbands and fathers.

Then there are, of course, my own parents, Joe and Brenda Howard. I would not be where I am today if it were not for their unconditional love and support. It is because of their example as well as their love and devotion to family that I have grown to so deeply value and appreciate the blessings of marriage and parenthood.

I must also thank my good friend Zuzana Urbanek for her editing, proofreading, and formatting expertise. She took on the monumental task of making sure that I didn't look like an idiot and, despite the overwhelming odds, did a superb job. Thanks, Z. This book never would have made it to print without you.

Most of all, I want to thank God who has blessed me with my incredible family and who put the people in my life who have helped me grow as a husband, father, and writer. I thank Him for the ability to write this book and the patience with which He has dealt with and restored me during the times in my life when my faith has wavered. I pray He will continue to guide me and teach me to be the man I must be for my wife and kids, as well as for the couples I strive to help.

– Kindred

Table of Contents

Introducing an
Average Caveman

I'm a self-proclaimed Doctor of Dadlosophy (a.k.a., a D.o.D). What is a *dadlosophy*? It's simply a father's take on life and parenthood—outlooks on the world developed from an average dad's perspective. Far from being the product of natural wisdom or intelligence, dadlosophies are, at least in my case, most often begotten through trial and error. I learn things the hard way. It's usually not until I've banged my head against a few walls that I start to figure things out. Don't believe me? Just ask my wife, Meredith.

What qualifies me to write this book? Well, let me be the first to say that I don't get into statistics or scientific methods. I'm not a licensed therapist, nor do I possess a degree in psychology. What I do bring to the table is eleven years of experience in the full-time ministry, during which I counseled people from every walk of life about all kinds of issues—including marriage and parenthood. I'm also a certified parenting coach (sounds impressive, doesn't it?). My greatest credential for writing this book, however, is simply this: I've been happily married to the same woman for the last fourteen years and have successfully loved my wife through multiple pregnancies. Together, Meredith and I are raising five children. My daughter, Emerson, is eight years old. My two oldest sons, William and Carson, are five and three respectfully. And my youngest sons, Samuel and Asher, are eleven-month-old twins.

Despite any "credentials" I may possess, believe me when I tell you that I write this book not with an arrogant belief that I have all the answers, but rather with a conviction that my experiences are not that different from those of most parents. I simply observe life, learn from my mistakes, and hopefully share some insights that moms and dads might find helpful. I find humor in parenthood that's inspired by reality. The dadlosophies I offer are tidbits of wisdom gained over the last few years.

Beginner's Parenthood

There are many stages to parenthood. This book focuses on the earliest: the decision to have kids, pregnancy, and common experiences after a new baby arrives. It's the stage commonly referred to as "beginner's parenthood," and which I call "Babyland." Specifically, this book is addressed to new mommies, soon-to-be mommies, and women who are thinking of becoming mommies. My goal is to offer some humor, encouragement, and what I hope are helpful tips that will enable new moms to better understand what's going on inside the heads and hearts of their male counterparts.

Why is understanding one's male counterpart so important? Well, as any new mom will discover, pregnancy and parenthood can place stress on a marriage. Sure, becoming a mom or dad is exciting and rewarding. The nine months of planning, dreaming, and preparing that lead up to the baby's arrival is an amazing time which most parents will look back on fondly. But the demands and life changes that accompany the voyage to parenthood aren't always easy. The differences between men and women often become magnified. A lack of understanding can lead to frustration, anger, and unnecessary conflict. In my own marriage as well as in many of those I've counseled, I've found that a woman will often point to a man's insensitivity and failure to communicate love and appreciation as the sparks that ignite female feelings of resentment. Hopefully, by helping women understand a bit more about where we "insensitive" men are coming from, I can arm new mommies with the knowledge they need to more effectively address their males' shortcomings. Simultaneously, I hope to encourage them with the realization that their new or soon-to-be daddies usually have no intention of making them feel underappreciated or neglected.

I believe that any man who takes the time to better understand how his wife thinks and why she feels what she feels not only becomes a more sensitive husband, he becomes a better father as well. Likewise, a mom who learns to better understand her husband and the mindset behind his comments and actions not only becomes a more loving wife, she also grows as a mother. Why? Spouses who understand one another tend to exhibit more acceptance, unconditional love, patience, and (when necessary) grace and forgiveness toward their significant other. Mutual understanding strengthens marriages, and strong marriages lay a foundation for great parenting.

Most pregnant mommies (especially if they are having their first child) spend valuable time reading books and articles and surfing the Internet for information that will help them comprehend what is happening during pregnancy. They want to understand what is going on inside their baby-carrying bodies. They will eagerly research to learn what they might encounter come delivery day and what to expect once baby arrives. But how many of these same moms take the time to learn what the pregnancy experience is like from a dad's perspective?

Don't get me wrong. I'm not complaining that dads don't get enough attention. After all, you moms are the ones carrying another human being inside your body. You're the ones who deserve to be pampered and taken care of. Still, if the Bible is true, then a man and woman who have come together to make a baby have, in a sense, become one flesh (Genesis 2:24). If that's the case, then taking time to understand what your soon-to-be dad is thinking and feeling actually falls fittingly into the "grasping what changes your body is undergoing" category. By helping mommies know what pregnancy and new parenthood look like from the testosterone-carrying side of the stadium, I intend to help minimize their frustration and lessen the chances of a husband needing to have his wife's flip-flop surgically removed from one of his bodily cavities.

So, Why *THIS* Book?

Why am I writing a book to mommies meant to help them better understand what new dads are thinking? Why not write a book to new daddies instead? Is it that I think new mommies and their inability to understand new daddies are the reason for all the conflicts that arise during pregnancy and parenthood? Am I implying that couples could end all their strife and fix all their problems if women would just care enough to really get to know us tragically misunderstood men? Of course not! In fact, I think the accusation that men often come across as insensitive and not working hard enough to meet their wives' emotional needs is quite fair. I'm not suggesting that women are the only ones who need to work on things, nor am I attempting to defend myself and my fellow males. I've simply chosen to accept the general reality that MEN DON'T READ PARENTING BOOKS! We read newspapers, financial statements, sports magazines, and literature related to our careers; but we rarely read about relationships or parenting.

Think about it, when was the last time your husband came home from work and asked, "Honey, has the latest issue of *Parenting Magazine* arrived? Doug at the office already read it, and he told me that this month's issue has a great article on crafts I can do with the kids."

By the same token, how often has the man in your life said, "Sweetie, if you could pick up a copy of Dr. Phil's latest book, I would really appreciate it. I heard he shares some great tips on how men can be more nurturing." Have I made my point yet?

Oh sure, your husband might occasionally read an article on marriage or parenting if *YOU* make him. But even then, he won't retain much. It's not that men don't care about being good parents or loving husbands; it's just that we don't put the same trust and value in someone else's written opinion or have the same sense of urgency that women do. Where women see a major relationship issue, men often see no problem at all. Where women see a huge marriage obstacle, men commonly see a minor marital glitch that can easily be fixed. It's not that we men don't value our marriages; it's just that we're arrogant (or stupid) enough to think we've got it covered. I guess it's in our genetic makeup. It's the same gene that leads us to believe that we don't need to stop for directions, can assemble things without reading the instructions, and can eventually get a broken-down car to start simply by raising the hood and looking at the gizmos underneath. We're "cavemen." We don't see the need to be "intellectuals" when it comes to relationships.

In short, I'm addressing you mommies because you'll actually read what I have to say. That's not to say that you should give up on reaching your cavemen, however. Trust me, there are things in this book that they should read or hear. But since cavemen aren't inclined to read relationship books, I'd suggest that you and I work together to try an indirect approach. We team up. I provide the written material, and you provide your most persuasive "Honey, if you love me, you'll listen while I read this to you" tone of voice. Together, maybe we can get some cavemen to sit and pay attention while you share a point or two that you want them to take note of. Who knows, maybe they'll laugh or hear something they agree with and think, "Huh, that book sounds like it might be kinda cool." With a little luck, maybe we can draw your cavemen in together. By the time they realize they're learning something worthwhile to help your relationship, they'll already be sold on the fact that the book is interesting and the guy who wrote it is twice as messed up as they are.

Reading Forward

Before proceeding to the first chapter, let me point out a couple of things regarding wording and structure. Throughout the book, I often use the terms *moms* and *wives*, the words *dads* and *husbands*, and the words *relationship* and *marriage* interchangeably. I realize, of course, that we live in a day and age when many couples who are not married have and raise children together. Many of these couples are very committed to one another and to their kids. Being an unmarried father doesn't necessarily mean one is a disengaged dad. While I personally believe that the institution of marriage is the best scenario in which to have and raise a child, I also acknowledge that there are unmarried couples who have and maintain strong, loving relationships. In my opinion, any couple devoted to loving one another and their kids, and striving to play an intricate part in their children's growth and development, is worthy of respect and admiration. Therefore, many of the things written in this book apply to most parents who take an active role in raising their children. I choose to use the terms I've mentioned interchangeably, not to exclude unmarried couples, but rather for simplicity's sake.

You will also note that most chapters include my personal stories. These accounts are meant to serve three purposes. First, they help me illustrate whatever point I might be making in the chapter. Second, they allow you to get to know me and my family, hopefully making the message more relatable and any suggestions I might make more trustworthy and applicable. Third, they serve as a living example of how the average caveman thinks. By reading about how I—a typical male—have perceived and experienced my wife's pregnancies and my own life as a young dad, you will hopefully pick up on some common trends and make connections between me and your own caveman. By sharing openly about myself, I hope that the mommies who read this will experience a few "Aha! That's just like my husband!" moments from which they can gain some encouragement and insight.

Finally, keep in mind that I am writing to a diverse audience. Not every scenario or characteristic I address will describe your particular caveman. So, note the sections that apply to your caveman, and glean what helpful information you can.

On a Practical Note

On a practical note, I have divided the book into three sections. Section 1, "Basic Caveman," includes chapters 1–3 and shares some foundational thoughts—basic principles about men that pregnant and new mommies could find useful when trying to better understand their cavemen. Section 2, "The Pregnancy Cave," includes chapters 4–7 and looks at how men perceive pregnancy and the events of delivery day. Section 3, "The Baby Cave," includes chapters 8–14 and addresses the male perspective on life once you bring your new baby home. Finally, the book concludes with some brief, closing thoughts from yours truly.

Each chapter is divided into shorter subsections. The purpose of the subsections is to give you brief portions of text that you can read quickly and at your convenience. After all, this book is intended for expecting and new mommies. If you're pregnant, then you already have a lot on your plate. You're probably reading various other books that answer questions like:

- How long will I keep vomiting more than a freshman during rush week?

- When will I stop rivaling the polar ice caps for overall level of water retention?

- If I killed my husband for doing this to me, is there any chance I could get off with just supervised probation?

In addition to all that research, you've got a nursery to decorate, baby showers to register for, car seats to pick out, and names to ponder, discard, and finally compromise on with your husband. You don't have a lot of time. Therefore, you need sections you can absorb quickly and easily. If you have time to read this book in long stretches, great. But I'm writing it with your busy schedule in mind.

If your little bundle of joy has already arrived, then you have even less time to read. Your waking hours are spent feeding babies, wiping fannies, bathing munchkins, longing for sleep, and scaring the pee out of your husband with exhaustion-induced mood swings that make him wonder if he should invest in a crucifix and a vile of holy water. Other than scanning the *Book of Revelation* to see if what you are going through might actually be the first stage of the Tribulation, you likely won't want to read anything that isn't short and sweet.

Parenthood Is Awesome

Make no mistake, both my wife and I believe that being a parent is the greatest thing on earth. It's challenging sometimes. There are moments when I'm sure I can't change one more diaper, referee one more argument over who got the biggest cookie, or deal with one more emotional meltdown from a three-year-old because Dad had the audacity to make a peanut butter and jelly sandwich differently than Mommy. But overall, there is no greater blessing in my life than my family. If, as a couple, you have decided to embark on the journey to mommy- and daddyhood, then I commend you and will be the first to say, "IT'S AWESOME!" Meredith and I have five kids who sometimes drive us to the brink of insanity, but they also bring a joy and meaning to our lives that, even in a book like this, cannot be fully expressed.

Again, mine are not the writings of a licensed psychologist or a professional therapist. But that's okay. I've found that, most of the time, we don't need professional counseling or a formal psychiatric evaluation. We just need someone we can talk to over a cup of coffee in order to realize that we're not alone. Other parents are trying to figure this thing out too. We're not the lone sinking raft adrift in a sea of people who've "got it together." We just need to hear some other parents' war stories to realize that we're all fighting the same battles. The things written in this book are not meant to be absorbed as if the reader were a patient in a psychologist's office. Rather, they're conversations between friends. It's just a bunch of war stories—simple dadlosophies meant to give new and expecting mommies the inside scoop on their everyday new or soon-to-be dad.

SECTION I:

Basic Caveman

Chapter 1:
The Prehistoric Mind

Generally speaking, men and women are programmed differently. They often don't see and interpret experiences and circumstances the same way. Males (a.k.a. cavemen) filter life through what I call the "prehistoric mind." Understanding a few things about how this prehistoric mind works can help pregnant and new mommies decode the male encryption, better enabling them to figure out where their caveman is coming from. Such decoding is key when you consider that it often can prevent a mom from pulling out her hair and slipping helplessly into husband-induced insanity.

A clearer understanding of the prism through which men see their surroundings usually better equips women to deal with a man's seemingly rude, insensitive, or strange behavior. It might even change a young mommy's perspective, leading her to actually appreciate the things her caveman is saying and doing because she can better grasp the heart and intention behind them.

Cavemen Aren't Dumb

First, some clarification is in order. When I refer to men as "cavemen" or having a "prehistoric mind," I am not in any way attempting to criticize or paint as intellectually lacking the members of my own gender. The truth is that I find the manner in which our modern culture often portrays husbands and fathers to be rather offensive and somewhat destructive. Husbands and fathers are commonly presented as the dummies in the family. While wives and mothers are often depicted as the real brains of the operation, keeping the family afloat and providing the household with its only intelligent parental direction, dads and husbands are often scripted to be little more than overgrown kids who constantly blow it, engage in unsuccessful schemes, tackle projects they can't handle, and generally spend most of their time screwing up.

A few years ago, one of the most popular shows on television was a sitcom called *Everybody Loves Raymond*. I enjoyed the show and often found it hilarious. But as much as I found the program entertaining, there was one aspect of the show that continually bugged me. Raymond—the main character, a husband, and the father of three—was each week depicted as a self-centered, insensitive boob who barely spent time with his kids and who wouldn't have been able to function if it weren't for his responsible wife, Debra. If Raymond's character had been the exception to how husbands and fathers are normally depicted, then it wouldn't have been a big deal. But the sad fact is that the show's depiction of "dumb dad Raymond" seems to be on par with how dads are commonly portrayed. According to the modern TV/commercial image, moms usually provide the real leadership in the family. They manage to hold it all together despite their husbands' selfishness, laziness, and overall lack of intellect. Dads are just a problem to be solved, a mistake to be reversed, an obstacle to be overcome, or a family joke that even the kids aren't expected to take too seriously. Sure, the stereotypical portrayal of dads might win a quick laugh on a sitcom or make for a funny commercial, but I can't help but feel that it also sends a more powerful negative message than many of us realize. How can we call young fathers to step up to the plate and be responsible, respectable, engaged dads who are positive role models for their children, when our culture is continually pounding them with images that suggest most "average" dads are the exact opposite?

I strongly reject the negative daddy stereotypes. I believe that most American fathers and soon-to-be dads are far better men than the Raymonds and Homer Simpsons of the world. When I use terms like "caveman" and "prehistoric" I'm simply using them to make a point: men tend to have a simpler, more straightforward view of the universe. It's not better than women's; it's not worse. It's not smarter; it's not dumber. It's just male.

When I write about understanding the prehistoric mind, I'm not implying that women have to dumb-down their way of thinking to comprehend men. Rather, I'm just pointing out that men generally approach things with a different mindset. We guys have a tendency to be ultra-logical, matter-of-fact, and normally less in touch with our emotions than women. When it comes to relationships, we generally proceed with the head more than with the heart (not always a good thing). Even when we follow our heart, it's usually only after the head has had its say in the matter and all possible ramifications of our actions (at least those we can think of) have been considered. Therefore, understanding how men think differently than women can prove valuable to an expecting or new mommy who might otherwise think her husband is just being an idiot. Of course, these tendencies aren't true of all men. But I'd say the above description applies to most of the dads I know.

Cavemen Grunt Logically

Most men deal in the logical. When a problem arises or is mentioned, we immediately look for a solution. After all, isn't that the *logical* thing to do when one becomes aware of a problem? We opt for an expedient answer that makes sense. One of the first things I had to learn as a husband is that, in my wife's world, logic occasionally carries only limited value. This was especially true during pregnancy. As men, we want to know if something makes sense, solves the problem, is practical, and so on. Expectant moms aren't always so concerned with such questions. They don't necessarily want the common sense answer. Instead, what they want is *encouragement*. Their bodies are undergoing physical changes that affect their moods, their habits, and their appearance. Such transformations can understandably lead to a lot of insecurity. Expecting mommies don't always want straightforward answers. Instead, they want their feelings validated. They aren't as interested in practicality as they are in positive reinforcement. Unfortunately, it takes most cavemen a while to figure out that, as new or soon-to-be dads, they sometimes need to abandon logic in favor of a more emotionally supportive approach. Even when they do figure it out, there's no guarantee that they'll know how to be supportive without making a few stupid comments first.

For instance, a woman who is several months pregnant is likely to get depressed about the way she looks (not that she should, but she does). She will then likely throw out a question to her caveman like, "Do I look like I've gained weight?" Now, for a man, this is like parachuting into the middle of a minefield. There is a way out; but if he doesn't watch his step, he'll be blown into so many pieces that all the king's horses and all the king's men will take one look at him and say, "Screw that! Let's try Humpty again."

If this is your caveman's first time as a soon-to-be father, then the likelihood of him avoiding an explosion is very low. He most likely will say something stupid even though he doesn't mean to. During my rookie pregnancy, my response to a weight question would have been something like: "Yes, Honey, you've gained some weight. But don't feel bad, that's to be expected; you're pregnant." BOOM! Massive explosion! Kindred has just won a night on the couch and a self-made peanut butter and jelly sandwich for dinner. But why? What's wrong with that answer? Isn't it logical? Isn't it true? Perhaps. But, once again, cavemen must learn that logic and truth aren't always what's called for in pregnancy world. We're trying to help. We just haven't yet learned what our expecting moms really want in a response.

A more experienced caveman, such as one who already has a kid, might respond to the same question with, "Yes, you've gained some weight; but you're still beautiful, and you'll lose it after the baby comes." BAM! His leg just got blown off. It's a bit better. He got further through the minefield than the rookie did. But he's still left dragging his bleeding body through the mud. He threw in some encouragement when he included the "you're beautiful" part; that was good. But he still acknowledged the weight. That's too much truth.

The thing most of us cavemen don't figure out until it's too late is that, nine times out of ten, you mommies already know the true answer to the question that you've asked us. You already know what's practical. After all, you're not stupid. We're not smarter than you. Most of the time, you're not asking us if you look like you've gained weight or been overly emotional lately because you want us to tell you the truth. No, you're asking us these things because you want us to say something that *makes you feel better* about the truth. Am I wrong?

An experienced veteran of the pregnancy wars—a dad who's lost a limb or two in the minefields before—usually comes closer to knowing what to say: "Oh Honey, you look beautiful. You've always been gorgeous, and you're even more gorgeous pregnant." Bingo! There you go. Minefield exited. He didn't say she hadn't gained weight; that would have insulted his wife's intelligence, made her feel patronized, and led to an explosion. No, he wisely just side-stepped the mine. He got out of the weight area altogether and just focused on how beautiful his wife is. He gave her an encouraging, reassuring response. And, as your caveman will hopefully learn, such responses are golden in and around Babyland.

Cavemen Mean Well

The key thing to remember, mommies, is that your caveman means well. He's not trying to be hurtful, unfeeling, or uncaring. It's just that, because your caveman views the world differently, he often misses the boat on why you actually asked your question or made a comment about the way you look, feel, act, and so on. You ask a question and want encouragement. He hears the question and thinks you want a logical answer. You make a comment wanting to be disagreed with. He hears the comment and thinks you want him to agree and then tell you what you could do to change things. You ask a "yes-no" question wanting him to say "no" regardless of his true opinion. He hears the question and thinks you want an honest answer. He's not trying to hurt your feelings or make you mad (although sometimes he will); he's just a typical caveman. His responses are a product of the prehistoric mind.

What I'm getting at is this: you have to help your caveman understand what you're really looking for when you ask a question, make a comment, or cry without warning. It will also help if you're willing to occasionally look past his boneheaded comments to find the good intentions buried beneath his seemingly insensitive words. If you don't, you might as well go ahead and build a bomb shelter in your bedroom because, trust me, you're going to be in for a lot of explosions.

Cavemen Like Control

Another key truth to understand about the prehistoric mind is that it has a strong need to comprehend what it encounters. Cavemen like routines. Get up, kiss the wife, leave the cave, hunt something, kill it, return to the cave, eat, have sex with the wife, sleep (preferably without having to talk after sex), get up the next day, do it again. When there's a routine, we men know what to expect. We're on top of the situation. That's how we like it. We don't necessarily mind a challenge; we just want to know we have some say over how we meet it.

While it might not be true of all men, I've found that most guys like predictability. This is especially true of dads. Even if a guy is an outside-the-box thinker or enjoys trying new things, he still wants to understand what he's dealing with. We guys like things in order. Generally speaking, we're most secure when the checkbook is balanced, the budget is adhered to, and plans go as scheduled. If we face an unexpected situation, we want it to be something that we at least have some idea of how to handle and, if necessary, fix. Most cavemen are not multitaskers. We like to attack a specific task or situation, deal with it, accomplish what needs to be done, and move on. We don't want to spin a lot of plates. We want to deal with one plate, clean it, put it in the cupboard, and then grab the next dish. In short, *WE LIKE TO FEEL IN CONTROL.*

The unfortunate reality for men is that pregnancy and parenthood lead to many unpredictable situations. Often, there are no quick fixes or simple solutions. Sometimes, there's no fix at all. There's nothing for a caveman to do except just be there and be supportive of his new mommy. Since we guys often feel inadequate until we've *done* something to improve a situation, "just being there" to listen and offer emotional support without doing anything to fix the problem can often leave us feeling confused, lost, overwhelmed, and frustrated. It's not our natural way. If a guy says something like, "Man, I can't stand my boss; I wish I had a different job," then, most of the time, his friends recognize that as an invitation to jump in with suggestions. They'll start giving him ideas for how he can better deal with his boss or find a better job. After all, didn't the guy bring up the problem because he wants help *solving* it? That's the way the prehistoric male mind works.

But that's not always how the post-prehistoric female mind works. What I had to learn early in my marriage (and only after continually frustrating my wife) is that a woman often shares a problem or the details of an unpleasant situation not because she wants her caveman to solve the problem, but rather because she wants him to listen to how she *feels* about the problem. She doesn't want her caveman to change her situation; she just wants the person she loves most in this world to validate her feelings with a comforting nod and a sincere comment like, "I can understand why you feel that way." Thus, when a woman says, "I can't stand my boss; I wish I had a different job," she *might* be inviting suggestions. But chances are she just wants her caveman to shut up and listen while she vents and gets out all of the frustration and anger she's feeling at that moment. After she's finished and calmed down, *then* she may want some practical suggestions. But not even that is a given. Once she's gotten all of her feelings off her chest, she might actually remember that she likes her boss, she enjoys her job, and it was just some particular situation or interaction that day that upset her and left her on the verge of tears.

This is very different from the way cavemen think. Even if a guy is smart enough to shut up and listen while a woman vents to him about a bad conversation or a challenging day, that doesn't mean he totally gets it. He still often finds himself staring dumbfounded at his wife's rapidly moving lips and wondering to himself:

- Is she asking me a question?

- Am I the one making her cry?

- Is that still English she's speaking?

- Am I expected to beat somebody up when she's finished?

I've actually seen Meredith talk herself through a problem without me ever having to say a word. She wants me there to hear her, but she doesn't need me to say anything. She'll go on and on until she feels better, then say "Thank you, Honey" and move on to something else. As a new husband, I couldn't figure out what I'd done. I would even feel insecure, believing I'd failed because I hadn't suggested or done more to correct her situation. But what I eventually learned is that sometimes being what a woman needs doesn't require any words or actions; it just means caring enough to look her in the eyes and listen.

It's hard for cavemen to get this at first because it means having to acknowledge their own lack of control. There is no set plan for dealing with a woman's emotions. The predictable, practical approach cavemen are so comfortable with is often uncalled for in the post-prehistoric female world. It's challenging for many men to learn the art of emotional support because it often doesn't require any outward action. You don't necessarily rush in to fix things. And that totally goes against a caveman's natural way of thinking.

Prehistoric Listeners

Finally, it may encourage you moms to realize something regarding the way cavemen listen. In the prehistoric world, it's not essential that a person look at others in order to listen to them. Listening while remaining engaged in an activity or looking at a television or computer screen is perfectly acceptable among men. In fact, we're pretty good at it.

Unfortunately, while this might be standard listening procedure among cavemen, I've found this kind of behavior to be a major violation of post-prehistoric female listening etiquette. It's also a major argument starter between husbands and wives. In my wife's world, listening means that you look directly at a person, make eye contact, and clearly communicate with your body language that the person has your undivided attention. You look up from your work. You stop staring at the television. In the female realm, it's not enough to hear and process what a person says. You've got to *appear to be listening.* It's not enough to listen to a person; you have to make that person feel listened to. A man's failure to look up from what he's doing or watching greatly offends and irritates women. And yet, many times, if a frustrated woman asks a seemingly inattentive male, "What did I just say?" her caveman can actually repeat it back to her verbatim. Why? Because he really was listening; he just wasn't doing it the female way.

My point is not that you aren't entitled to have your caveman stop what he's doing and look at you while you talk to him. Certainly, you are. Rather, I'm just pointing out that your caveman may very well be listening to you when you're tempted to think that he's not. If you need him to do more to make you feel listened to, then tell him. But hold off before you get your feelings hurt or get mad thinking he's not listening or that he doesn't care. You may very well find that he is and he does. In his mind, he just knows that he can successfully listen to you while tracking his fantasy football team at the same time.

Talk to Your Caveman

Communication is key. If you're upset or concerned about something that really needs to change, then tell your caveman. The prehistoric mind longs to understand and come up with a plan to fix problems. On the other hand, if what you're feeling is just a passing emotion, then let him know that too. Help him see that there are certain things he can't control or fix. Sometimes, he just needs to be there to let you vent, cry, talk, babble, growl, or whatever.

Like you, your new or soon-to-be father is entering a whole new world by becoming a parent. He needs help figuring things out. So don't fall into the trap of just getting mad because your caveman isn't being what you think he should be. Talk to him and let him know what you need. It might take every ounce of strength he can muster to resist using a prehistoric approach, but at least with your help he can better know how to meet your new-mommy needs.

Chapter 2:
Land of the Lost

A couple of years ago, Meredith and I took our kids to visit a corn maze. A corn maze is just what its name suggests: a maze cut out of ten-foot-high stalks of corn. People—of their own free will, mind you—pay their hard-earned money to get lost among its rows of husks.

If you think about it, a corn maze is really a monument to rural capitalism. Where else but in America can a down-on-his-luck farmer survey his field; say to himself, "Ya know, if I took my John Deere and plowed me a maze in that there corn, I bet they's people from the city dumb enough to give me money to walk through it"; then proceed to rake in big bucks from folks who are eager to spend an autumn afternoon meandering in and out of corn? Somewhere, the agricultural entrepreneur who came up with this idea is sitting at a table, counting his money, and laughing it up alongside the guy who got rich proving Americans are gullible enough to buy bottled water.

I can honestly say that I have never had a burning desire to visit a corn maze. But, because my kids wanted to go, my wife and I loaded up the minivan and headed north into the southern Appalachian Mountains. One thing I quickly learned: don't go to a Georgia corn maze in early September. It's too freakin' hot! If you're just dying to navigate crops, hold off until mid-October when the weather is more bearable. Our family entered the corn maze just after the sun reached its noon-time peak (a tactical mistake on my part). As I led my children into the agricultural labyrinth, I was handed a map that, in theory, would help us find our way out. It proved useful for all of ten minutes before my family and I found ourselves hopelessly lost. As sweat poured out of our rapidly dehydrating bodies, our tiny band wandered aimlessly among the ears of corn. Our only remaining connection to civilization was the occasional sound of another father a few rows over screaming, "Where the heck do we turn left? The map says we should turn left!" Clueless about how to get out and growing more irritable by the minute, I couldn't help but think to myself, *C'mon! The last time people got this off course, it was after an entire sea parted and the group's leader had been entrusted with Ten Commandments.*

As Meredith and I grew more and more frustrated (each blaming the other for failing to correctly read the map), my children proceeded to add to the "fun" with comments like "Daddy, I'm tired. Daddy, I'm hot. Daddy, please carry me. Daddy, can I pee in the corn?" (That reminds me: my apologies to anyone who ate any of that year's North Georgia corn crop.) Of all people, it was my daughter, Emerson, who finally led us out. Relieved to escape the dusty heat of *Hee-Haw* hell, we rushed to the lone concession stand and loaded up on Gatorade and water as fast as we could. A few snacks and one hayride later, and we were back in our minivan—our first (and hopefully last) corn maze experience behind us.

Pregnancy Is a Corn Maze

The point in sharing my corn maze experience is simply this: for cavemen, life with a pregnant woman or new mommy is like living in a corn maze. We're lost! We men are meandering down dusty trails without a readable map and in desperate need of help. No doubt about it, when it comes to pregnancy and early parenthood, men *WANT* understandable directions. We want women to tell us what they need us to be and do.

I know that the notion of men wanting directions goes against women's conventional thinking regarding men. Women generally view men as having a natural aversion to asking for help. To a great extent, they're right. Take driving for instance. Most men refuse to admit when they're lost. While our well-meaning female counterparts are politely suggesting that we stop and ask directions, we guys fail to see the need. Why stop at a convenience store for navigational help when every guy knows that his testosterone-fueled instincts will eventually kick in and put him right back on course?

Then there are the arts of assembling, mounting, and fixing things. If something needs to be fixed, modified, or built from scratch, male pride often convinces cavemen that mastering the situation falls within our realm of abilities. Who cares if we've never been trained to do it or even seen it done? We're men, for cryin' out loud! Just hand us a Phillips screwdriver and some duct tape, then get out of our way. Why worry if electricity or propane is involved? We know what we're doing. Why spend all that money on fire extinguishers? We'll probably never need them. I've known guys who believe that they can purchase something that requires assembly, take one look at the picture on the box, and then successfully construct it after paying only minimal attention to the written instructions. Directions may be helpful, but they're not essential—at least not in the prehistoric mind. The way we men see it, if we encounter any problems putting something together or tackling a maintenance project, it's probably because the manufacturer is an idiot who failed to produce a quality product or provide clear directions rather than due to any incompetence on our part.

Ah ... Communication

While men's pride often does result in a severe case of ill-advised-self-sufficiency syndrome, our propensity for self-reliance tends to apply only to those areas about which we think we know something. True, the fact that we think we know more than we do means that our pride surfaces quite often. But there are subjects about which we cavemen acknowledge that we're clueless and in desperate need of guidance. Most often, these areas are directly related to our relationships with women. When it comes to women, we know we need help. Unfortunately, while women normally long for us to seek directions when lost on a road trip or assembling a piece of baby furniture, they often expect men to already know what to do when it comes to relationships and understanding females. This expectation inevitably leads to conflicts and frustrations that incline men to want to retreat and escape rather than advance and conquer. Most men don't want to upset their wives; they just need help figuring out how not to.

In a nutshell, what I am talking about is clear, concise communication. A man needs to be open and humble. He should communicate to his wife in a calm, non-combative tone that he is trying to be sensitive and helpful but that he legitimately can't figure out what she needs him to be. Conversely, a woman needs to understand and appreciate the fact that her caveman is trying. She needs to recognize that pregnancy and parenthood are new ballgames for him, and she's going to have to tell him some of the rules.

As anyone who's ever been in a relationship knows, men and women have a hard time understanding one another and patiently accepting one another's differences. Admittedly, we guys are often the source of the problem because of our thick skulls and repeated inability to "get it." We function best in a simplified world. We long for a land where "Yes" means yes, "No" means no, and a woman's affirmative answer to the question, "Honey, is it okay if I go out with the guys tonight?" actually means that we can hang with our buddies for an evening without getting the silent treatment and facing a night of involuntary celibacy when we get home. As cavemen, we don't even like to talk if we don't have to. If a grunt or nod will suffice, then that's what we prefer to go with.

Early in my marriage, I learned that women are different. Emotionally, my wife is much more complicated than I am. Her female English is far more sophisticated than my male English. Whereas male English consists of words that mean exactly what they say, female English is more of a tonal language. I had to figure out that it's not enough for me to hear what Meredith says; I have to listen for what she actually *means*. Thus, when I ask Meredith if she's cool with me taking off for a few hours to spend the evening with the guys, I have to remain aware that "Yes" doesn't always mean yes, "No" doesn't always mean no, and "It's okay if you go out with your friends" sometimes means "No, it's not okay; in fact, how insensitive of you even to ask such a question! You'd better figure out where you screwed up fast and do some serious groveling, you jerk; or you won't have sex again until just after the Democrats nominate Rush Limbaugh for president!"

I find that this pattern is fairly consistent for most couples I know. In most relationships, men and women often have a hard time communicating; a fact that's unfortunate when you consider that the one rarely ever intends to hurt or frustrate the other. Throw in the emotional and hormonal (in the woman's case) rollercoaster ride known as pregnancy, and you've got the potential for some majorly explosive run-ins.

If you can identify with my wife's frustration at my early failures to pick up on her signals, then let me reassure you that your baby's father is not that unusual. He's not crazy. He's not trying to be a jerk. He hasn't stopped loving you or believing that you're beautiful. And, rest assured, he's not trying to ignore you or be intentionally insensitive to your needs. Nope, he's just a caveman. He's just as excited and scared as you are at the prospect of raising another human being. Ultimately, he's simply a prehistoric-minded dude who's trying his best to figure out what it means to be a husband and a father.

Just the Facts, Ma'am

Another major obstacle to maintaining healthy communication is the fact that men and women tend to interact differently and with different expectations. Once again, the core issue is the basic differences between the prehistoric and the post-prehistoric minds. Take, for example, phone conversations. With the exception of business calls, my longest phone calls usually last between thirty seconds and two minutes. I'm on the phone just long enough to know who I'm talking to, relay or receive any relevant information, find out if I am expected to be anywhere at a later time as a result of the phone call, and, if so, when and where I am supposed to be. Beyond that, I have no reason (nor desire) to stay on the phone any longer. It's short and sweet—a cell phone company's nightmare—no going over my minutes.

Women, on the other hand, are the reason cell phone company executives own vacation homes in The Bahamas. They can talk on the phone for hours and with no tangible objective. I can get off the phone after a forty-five second exchange and tell you exactly what has been or will be accomplished because of my talk. My wife, by comparison, can walk in the house on her cell phone, remain engaged in the same conversation while she unpacks her groceries, keep talking as she prepares an entire dinner, and not hang up until food is on the table and the kids have washed their hands. After all that, if I ask her what she and her friend were discussing, she's likely to say something like, "Oh, Sylvia (or Sandra, or Angela, or Stacy...) was just telling me about her day."

Women talk about experiences and feelings. Men will talk about experiences too, but usually only those that involve work, sports, food, or something that baffles us about our wives. Rarely do we talk about feelings unless we're in a doctor's office and the conversation centers around our colon. Women want to get in touch with the emotions they experience. Men just want the relevant facts.

As I see it, the problem with inter-gender communication is that men make the mistake of trying to interact with women the same way they do with other men. Women, conversely, make the mistake of interpreting a man's "just the facts ma'am" attitude as being an incredible lack of caring. That's because no woman would communicate that way unless, well, she didn't care. While some men certainly may be guilty of not caring enough, most have no such intention. Your caveman is usually not trying to blow you off or reduce your feelings to a list of dos and don'ts; he's just making the mistake of using a male approach instead of one that's female-friendly.

Now We Know We're in a Corn Maze

How does all this play out for expecting and new mommies? Simple: pregnancy and early parenthood are definitely areas where most men recognize that they are outside their areas of expertise. Even if he's cocky enough to think he knows what he's doing early on, a man will usually come to the conclusion that he needs his wife to help him know how to answer a whole array of questions.

- How do I meet the emotional needs of my pregnant wife?

- What's the correct response to my wife who's jacked up on hormones and starts crying because I walked by her in the bathroom without telling her that I love her?

- How do I approach my wife with my concern that we're spending too much money on baby clothes without sending her over the edge emotionally or making her think I don't love our unborn child?

- How should I respond when my expectant mommy is sobbing for no apparent reason, nauseous with morning sickness, upset about something that has never bothered her before, or laughing uncontrollably in a scary, mad-scientist sort of way?

Many times, women erroneously assume that men should know what to do or say. Trust me, we don't. We need and, if we're smart, will welcome your direction (especially where pregnancy and new babies are involved). Tell us what to do. Sure, we should eventually figure out some things. Even preschoolers learn how to write their own names after a while. You shouldn't have to keep covering the same ground over and over. But initially, we're clueless. We're likely to offend you or hurt your feelings with our inability to naturally tune in to your needs as young moms. My advice is to just tell us. Give us the directions.

If your caveman does something that hurts you or leaves you feeling disheartened or misunderstood, then, of course, you need to let him know. But go into the conversation realizing that his intentions were probably to help you rather than make you feel unimportant.

Walk Us through the Stalks

You're an awesome woman who's about to become (or just became) a spectacular mom. You deserve to be treated right! You deserve to have your emotional and physical needs met. You're entitled to a man who is right there by your side, fighting day in and day out to make your role as a mother easier by helping and encouraging you. Fortunately, most cavemen want to give you just that. But you're not a piece of baby furniture waiting to be assembled. We can't just look at the picture on the box. This time, we know we need help. At least in the beginning, we just need some facts—some straightforward instructions that help us know what you need us to be. Hopefully, in a relatively short amount of time, we'll learn to be more in tune with your emotional needs without you having to walk us through the rows of stalks. Until then, most likely, your caveman is sweating in a corn maze.

Chapter 3:
Cro-Magnon Appreciation

Here's a news flash: men can be insensitive. Shocking, I know. Take a moment to gather yourself and recover if you need to. Are you okay yet? Ready to read on? Good. Let's continue.

As a caveman, let me be the first to admit that, yes, we can be self-centered and hurtfully oblivious to how our better halves are feeling. This unfortunate fact can be especially detrimental during pregnancy and early parenthood. Wives (and especially moms) don't want to feel taken for granted. You want to feel appreciated. The truth is, most men actually do appreciate their new moms more than they express. We guys recognize that, for all the concerns we have as soon-to-be dads, expectant mothers have it a lot tougher. You gals are the ones who put up with all the nausea and backaches that accompany pregnancy. You're the ones who will spend your last trimester unable to see your own feet as you waddle about like the Penguin contemplating his next move against Batman. Once baby arrives, you'll be the ones waking up throughout the night to let a human parasite latch onto your breast to suck the life out of you. No doubt about it, for all the challenges we face as dads, moms are the real heroes.

In fact, I have long held to the theory that if men had the babies everyone would be an only child. That's because most of us guys would be arrogant enough to think that we could handle pregnancy—*ONCE*. But about the time we faced that first bout of morning sickness or noticed our ankles swelling up like softballs, we'd be begging God to kill us and swearing "Never again!" While women suck it up and go, barely even complaining—only asking for the occasional back rub or troubling us for the once-a-week late night run to the grocery store—we men would be reminding every soul within moaning distance of the walk through hell we were enduring. Can you imagine a suburb full of pregnant men? Not since the Angel of Death made his midnight trek through Egypt has such a cry of agony risen toward the heavens. Let's not even talk about contractions. Heck, if I eat a burrito, I'm in the bathroom groaning for twenty minutes. And if all that weren't enough, just imagine the look on any guy's face as some doctor pokes and prods his private parts, only to inform him that he's dilated ten centimeters. Second child? I think not. We men would have one kid, rush to get vasectomies faster than you can say "Supercuts," then gather at our favorite bar to outdo one another with labor stories rivaling your granddad's account of the Korean War.

Yes, you women deserve our admiration. You grow other people inside your own bodies, then, endure unimaginable pain while these same little folks kick, push, and rip their way out. Following the birth, women become baby feeding factories, awakening every two hours to make sure that the milk they're supplying continually meets their baby's demand. Moms are bitten, spit up on, scratched, and kicked. They can't sleep, can't get comfortable, and can't escape the ruthless hormones that bombard their bodies. And yet, somehow, despite the physical hardships and ever-decreasing number of showers, you moms still end up looking beautiful and seeming remarkably in control.

Appreciation Is a Valid Expectation

Appreciation is a valid expectation. You're certainly not being unreasonable to want your caveman to acknowledge with words and actions that he recognizes all you're going through to carry and care for his baby. Some men are good at expressing such appreciation for their wives. That's awesome! Good for them. They are great examples for the rest of us to follow. But many men I know aren't. While most of the guys I talk to truly are thankful for their wives and all they are doing, they tend to fall short of adequately making their wives *feel* appreciated. The explanation for this is pretty simple. We men tend to be selfish boneheads. A new daddy can easily lose sight of how awesome his new mom is because he gets too focused on his own concerns. He's too busy battling his own exhaustion, dealing with his own emotions, or nursing his own hurt feelings after his hormonally-charged pregnant wife yelled at him for forgetting to buy the Oreos she's been craving all day.

Men also come up short because they fail to properly read their wives' demeanor. Cavemen often fail to recognize their wives' anger, sadness, frustration, or emotional distance as an expression of feeling unappreciated. They think it's another unexplainable twist or turn on the hormonal rollercoaster known as pregnancy, or perhaps a product of new-mommy sleep deprivation. Once again, straightforward communication is necessary. If your caveman is ever going to realize that you feel taken for granted or under-valued, chances are you are going to have to tell him.

Be Encouraged, Mommies

New and expecting mommies should be encouraged by two things. First, know that any frustration you're experiencing from feeling underappreciated is not unusual. Odds are, you're not married to the most insensitive man on the face of the earth.

Second, if your caveman loves you as much as I'm willing to bet he does, then trust me, he wants you to know how much you mean to him and to feel appreciated. Often, when men seem most distracted and insensitive, it isn't because we don't care. Rather, it actually stems from the fact that we love you and our baby. We cavemen see it as our role to take care of our families. We want our families to feel secure. More specifically, we want to make sure that the future is secure—financially, emotionally, spiritually (if you're a person of faith), and otherwise. Ironically, often it's because we love you and our baby that we become too engrossed in life's concerns and unwittingly fail to tend to your emotional needs.

Learning that his wife is having a baby causes a caveman to make an assessment of himself. His mind inevitably mixes all the pride and euphoria of becoming a dad with all the fears and insecurities concerning his ability to raise another human being. Prior to learning you're pregnant, your caveman had the luxury of still believing that he had plenty of time to grow up, become responsible, come up with a financial plan, kick his bad habits, and so on. But now things have changed. Now fatherhood is on the horizon. Time's up—the alarm clock is ringing and he's got less than nine months to hit the snooze button. It's time to get his act together, and he knows it. The scary part for him is that he's not always exactly sure how. Such men often find themselves pondering questions like:

- How are we going to make it on just one salary or pay for daycare?

- How does one set up a financial plan for the future and start saving for college?

- Do I need more life insurance?

- How can I finally be as disciplined as I need to be?

- How are we going to afford all the extra things we need for a baby?

- How can I continue to pursue my career and be there for my wife and child?

Your caveman might not admit it, but the truth is that he may be feeling a lot of anxiety over whether or not he's ready to be the man he feels he needs to be in order to give you and his child the security he longs to provide. As much as we dads try to appear like we're holding it all together, in reality, we're facing many of the same fears and insecurities as you moms. We wonder if we'll be a good parent. We worry about what to do if "Plan A" doesn't work. We obsess over how we'll take care of our family if this or that happens. In short, we are at times basket cases—and we don't even have the excuse of pregnancy hormones.

If you think your caveman has temporarily forgotten about you or doesn't see what you're going through, you could be right, so feel justified in letting him know how you feel. Just know that his insensitivity and forgetfulness may be due in large part to his own fears and insecurities. Too often, we men fail to put our worries on hold so that we can devote the emotional attention necessary to ensure that the young mom in our lives still feels loved and appreciated. Our love and affection for our wives hasn't gone anywhere; we've just committed the all-too-common sin of burying it under a mound of practical considerations.

Trust and a Little Slack

So, what can a woman do given that Cro-Magnon levels of appreciation often aren't enough? Well, once again, I must stress the fact that I am no psychologist or licensed therapist. Still, as a former minister, certified parenting coach, and veteran husband and father, I have helped a number of young couples work through relationship and parenting issues. What I suggest is this: tell your caveman exactly how you're feeling, preferably in a tone that doesn't sound like you're attacking him. (Remember chapter 2? Cavemen need directions.) Of course, this can be challenging—especially when you're tired, angry, or fed up with his apparent lack of understanding. But this is where choosing to trust your caveman can prove invaluable. Trust that, in his heart of hearts, he really does appreciate and love you. The real problem isn't that he doesn't care how you feel, but that he's dropped the ball on meeting your emotional needs—and he most likely didn't mean to.

Also, be prepared to cut him some slack. This doesn't mean that you excuse or ignore his lack of sensitivity; it just means that you realize you're dealing with a prehistoric mind and you're prepared to meet your caveman where he is. Emotionally charged statements like, "You don't love me," or "You don't appreciate me," if not accompanied by some examples of things that have made you feel this way and practical direction on what he can do differently, will likely only confuse and frustrate your caveman, leading to more conflict and hurt feelings. Don't forget that cavemen are "doers." We want practical solutions to fix problems.

Your caveman can't read your mind. Tell him what you require to feel appreciated and valued. Otherwise, even with the best of intentions, he's liable to get it wrong. He might think you need him to say something when really all you need is for him to listen. He might think you want him to bring you flowers when what you'd really like is a shoulder massage. He might decide to take you to dinner when what you were hoping for was a five minute phone call from work to check on you, tell you he was thinking of you, and let you know that he loves you. Sure, when you first point out things to your caveman that have hurt your feelings or left you feeling forgotten he might react with defensiveness (probably because he loves you and he doesn't want to believe that he hurt you), but most likely he'll soon come around and sincerely want to work harder to make you feel happy, appreciated, and secure.

Find the Sincerity

Finally, I recommend that you look past your caveman's outward mistakes to find his inner sincerity. Occasionally, when I've counseled couples, I hear a wife say something along the lines of, "He's just doing what I want him to do now because I told him what to do. He's not doing it because *he wants to*. It doesn't count because it's not sincere."

While I can certainly understand why a wife might feel this way, in most cases, I disagree. It's true that your caveman might not totally understand why you need him to behave a certain way in order to make you feel loved and appreciated. But I would argue that the real test of his affection is this: *DOES HE DO IT ANYWAY?* Once you've made it clear to him what you need him to say, do, not say, or not do, does he try to follow through even though it might be something he never would have picked up on without your help? If so, it at least shows that he's taken you seriously and that he wants to be what you desire, even if he doesn't totally "get it" yet. If your caveman loves you, his desire to act in a way that makes you feel appreciated will usually precede his ability to understand why you need it.

Of course, you want your caveman to eventually understand *WHY* you need what you do without you having to explain it to him. And he will. Eventually, he'll graduate to that level—some get there faster than others. But, in the beginning, you may need to let him get away with just the outward expressions of love.

Don't underestimate how frustrating it can be for him when trying to figure out how to make you feel happy and appreciated. Just when he thinks he's got it figured out, you feel you need something different. One day you need him to patiently embrace your indecisiveness as you try to decide what shade of pink or blue would look best in the nursery. The next day (or minute) you might need a hug or for him to quietly hold you as you cry for no reason he can understand. And the next you might need him to reassure you that the fact he forgot to kiss you goodbye before he left home that morning doesn't mean he's considering leaving you. Add to all of that the fact that, nine times out of ten, you want him to figure out what he should do without you having to tell him, and you can begin to see that, for a caveman, knowing how to adequately express his appreciation for his wife can seem slightly harder than winning the National Spelling Bee.

The Good News

The good news is that your caveman loves you and appreciates you more than he knows to let on. He's not the mega-jerk he sometimes seems. He's average. He's a normal new or soon-to-be dad. He means well. Eventually, he'll get better at picking up on what his pregnant or new mommy needs. So don't worry. He'll get better. Your guy is nothing more than a typical caveman.

SECTION II:

The Pregnancy Cave

Chapter 4:
The Hormonal Tiger

History teaches us that the caveman was rugged. He rose early, gnawed the remaining meat off of the previous night's bone for breakfast, then left for the day without showering or shaving. He hunted, killed his prey, celebrated with friends over its fallen carcass, then dragged or carried it back to the cave. He was a warrior for his tribe, the defender of his family, the ruler of his world. He took what he wanted and threatened with physical harm anyone who dared stand in his way. He was ugly, crude, foul-odored, and violent—and he liked it that way.

Fear the Cat

But even the rugged and hardened caveman dared not cross one creature. Even this battle-sharpened gladiator of the prehistoric wilderness was careful to steer clear of one ferocious and dreaded beast—*the saber-toothed cat!* Why? The saber-toothed cat was a killer—a devourer of cavemen. No matter how powerful or skilled a caveman might be, if left alone to face the claws and long, protruding fangs of a raging saber-toothed cat, he was sure to be ripped apart. Although there may be little historic evidence to prove it, I would imagine that prehistoric cavemen spent many a night sitting around a fire and talking about ways to avoid a one-on-one encounter with this horrifying monster.

Of course, that was thousands of years ago. Saber-toothed cats no longer walk the earth. Unless you're reading this on the African savanna or in a jungle hut somewhere in rural India, you're probably not too concerned about a large predator jumping out of the brush and eating you. Still, for your twentieth-century caveman, there is something he fears every bit as much as his ancestors did the saber-toothed cat. No, it's not a four-legged creature that eats human flesh. If it were, he would at least have the option of killing it. Rather, it's a much less tangible but equally ferocious predator: *PREGNANT MOMMY HORMONES!*

Much of men's confusion during pregnancy comes from the fact that we don't understand the hormonal changes going on in a woman's body. We can see the physical changes that occur during pregnancy, but we have no way of gauging what's going on inside our soon-to-be mommies. Unlike the ancient cavemen who at least knew where they might run into a saber-toothed killer, we men are often unable to accurately predict when the hormonal tiger might pounce and rip us to shreds. We may not sit around late-night fires discussing how to stay out of the path of this potential man-eater, but we do discuss it around office water coolers or over beers at our favorite pub.

Hello, Christine

Pregnancy and motherhood aside, it seems to me that women have a love-hate relationship with hormones. On the one hand, you're mortal enemies. Every twenty-eight days or so, hormones swoop in on women like Lex Luthor unleashing a barrage of kryptonite on Superman. What follows is an intense battle waged by females for control of their own bodies. For women, it's a physically exhausting war that is fought every month. For men, it's a terrifying spectacle rivaled only by scenes from *The Exorcist*.

On the other hand, hormones also provide women with the ultimate "get out of jail free" card—a consistent "not guilty by reason of insanity" plea that men feel powerless to counter. No matter what a woman yells, says, breaks, throws, curses, or threatens with physical harm while going through her monthly episode, hormones provide women with a pass few guys dare to challenge. The way men see it, if a relationship is a toll gate, then a woman filled with hormones is like an out-of control driver behind the wheel of an SUV, ramming through the barrier at full speed and never stopping to drop her dollar in the slot.

Meanwhile, men sit there like the helpless toll collectors. All we can do is watch the destruction from our pitiful little booths. We didn't see the SUV coming until it was already on top of us. It hit so fast and with so much fury that we didn't have time to raise the gate or get the license plate number. We just stand there, staring aimlessly into the distance, as that SUV goes howling down the highway. The police might show up and ask us what happened, but it won't do much good. Even though we had a front row seat for the whole thing, we're still not exactly sure what we saw. One moment it was a lovely day, minivans and Volvos politely parading through our toll gate. Then, without warning, Stephen King's *Christine* came barreling out of nowhere, annihilating everything in its path. Yep, that's kind of what it's like for a man whose wife is full of raging hormones. Even though he's often the object of her fury, he rarely knows for sure what he did to bring it on.

Lightning Strikes

Now consider all the hormones that assault a woman's body during pregnancy and the first few months of motherhood. From a man's perspective, it's like witnessing PMS on steroids! I remember when Meredith was pregnant. One moment she was smiling and happy, dreaming about what our child would look like and all the great things he or she would grow up to be. The next she'd be in tears, convinced she would accidently leave the kid at Walmart or forget to feed it for a week.

Then there were the times she'd get upset at me. I often have a hard enough time figuring out why my wife is mad at me when she's not pregnant. You can imagine the challenge I faced once a few extra baby-making hormones got thrown into the mix. If I was quiet too long, she thought I obviously must not love her anymore. If I spoke but at the wrong time, she thought I obviously must not love her anymore. If I spoke at the right time but said the wrong thing, then, you guessed it, she thought I obviously must not love her anymore. If I complimented the way she looked, she accused me of thinking she was so unattractive that I felt compelled to say something to make her feel better. If I went more than an hour without telling her she's beautiful, she reasoned that I must think she's fat and ugly. Commercials made her cry. Music made her cry. Silence made her cry. *I made her cry*! Oh, it was loads of fun—hours and hours of at-home entertainment.

The fact is, pregnant women aren't storms that can be tracked on radar and predicted. They're the lightning strikes that come out of nowhere. Men might be aware there's a storm in the area, but we don't know when or where a bolt will shoot out of the sky and fry us like an onion ring. For men, being with a pregnant woman is like being outdoors in a thunderstorm for nine months. All the while we're standing on an aluminum roof and holding a five iron high above our heads. We know we're gonna get zapped, and there's nothing we can do to stop it. We can't fix whatever it is that's tossing our wives' emotions all over the place. We just have to ride out the storm and hope we'll somehow live to tell (or write) about it.

Of course, the hormones don't stop doing their thing once little baby arrives; they just switch gears. Once an infant is on the scene, mommy's body goes into high breast-milk-producing mode. Throw in the accompanying sleep deprivation that mommy endures (especially if she's nursing), and a woman's hormonally-fueled emotions occasionally consume her.

Then there are the frustrations a woman experiences simply from having her whole world turned upside down— especially if it's her first baby. This woman, who not that long ago was free to leave the house, go to work, see friends face-to-face, and have a life outside of Babyland, now becomes the indentured servant of a self-centered and demanding (albeit lovable) gnome who dominates her schedule, is oblivious to her pain, and couldn't care less if she hasn't slept in a week and needs "just a few hours to herself." Add it all up and it's no wonder mommy is, shall we say, a little on edge.

Why Bring Up Hormones?

At this point, you mommies might be quite irritated with me. After all, hormones can be a very sensitive issue for women. Maybe you think I'm a jerk for even bringing it up. Many of you might be saying to yourselves:

"What the heck do you know about hormones, Kindred? You're a guy. You've never had to deal with what it's like to have a baby or be an exhausted young mommy! What are you complaining about! Have you ever shot something the size of a watermelon out of YOUR body? Is anyone sucking on YOUR boobs so hard you can feel your eyeballs sliding backwards into your skull? Are you stuck with stretch marks that look like some pot-head from the '60s tried to tie-dye YOUR abdomen? Unless you've recently pooped a football or been stalked by a midget vampire who latches onto YOUR breasts every two hours to drain YOU dry, I'd suggest you quit all your whinin' and moanin' about a woman's hormones before I have no choice but to hunt you down and beat you to a pulp with the very laptop you typed this garbage on!"

Touché. You have a point. But keep in mind, my purpose is not to critique pregnant mommies. Rather, my goal is to give you the caveman's perspective. Once again, my hope is that by providing you with a bit of the prehistoric take on things, I might prevent you from clubbing your caveman to death with your breast pump or strangling him with the cord to your baby monitor. Given that the hormonal changes and the intense mood swings they elicit are such a huge part of mommyhood, it seems to me that I would be remiss if I did not address them, even if by broaching the subject I am, indeed, risking the wrathful retaliation of offended mommies.

61

Afraid of Ourselves

The fact of the matter is that most men experience a sense of shock and awe when standing face to face with the mysterious hormonal tiger. Interestingly, I find that women often can't understand why we cavemen have such a hard time dealing with a pregnant woman's emotionalism. After all, we know that a pregnant woman is full of raging hormones, so why can't we guys just roll with it?

Well, part of the problem is that we're scared of ourselves. That is to say, we're scared of our own inability to understand how a woman's body works. Once again, this takes us back to the prehistoric mind. Part of us feels like we should be able to prevent a woman's emotional meltdowns. It has to do with our desire to control things. Whereas women often view one of their emotional episodes or drastic mood swings as simply a natural part of pregnancy, men view these episodes as the result of something that could have been avoided. Men see it as their job to find what causes the flow of tears or the sudden angry outburst and fix it. We're wired to believe that if our wives cry, get upset, are mad, or so on, then they must be alerting us to something they want us to change. There must be something we can do to ensure that our new moms feel happy and content from here on out. But this is often not the case. Sometimes a woman just needs to vent, cry, yell, express her frustration, or just unload. That's just the nature of it.

What we cavemen have a hard time grasping is the notion that this is okay. One of the things cavemen need to embrace (and, again, this goes against the natural instinct of the prehistoric mind) is that a woman's occasional emotional swings and (dare I say) tirades don't always mean that a husband is failing. Sometimes, they just mean a woman's pregnant, tired, overwhelmed, or all of the above.

Confessions of a Bonehead

All that being said, I would be giving us guys too much credit if I didn't acknowledge that, yes, sometimes we are boneheads who inflame the problem by not thinking. I suppose it's part of our DNA. The prehistoric caveman, after all, discovered fire. Is it any wonder that we modern cavemen are so good at saying and doing things that can fuel one?

Take, for instance, an episode that occurred during one of Meredith's early pregnancies. A few weeks after we learned we were expecting, Meredith and I were invited to visit my aunt and uncle at their new lake house just outside of Columbia, South Carolina. It sounded great! After all, my wife loves my aunt, so how could it not be a perfect scenario? We'd enjoy a day at the lake while soaking up all the attention of being the young couple expecting a baby. I was about to learn, however, that when your wife is pregnant, there are no relaxing days by the lake. That's because your wife can't relax. She's carrying another human being in her belly, for cryin' out loud. She's ten degrees hotter than everyone else. She's tired. Her back aches. Nausea and vomiting have joined brushing teeth and the *Today* show as part of her morning routine. And, as Meredith occasionally pointed out to me, her body is working harder than that of someone who is running up a mountain backwards. Any appearance that her husband, a selfish non-pregnant male, is simply sitting and taking it easy, can potentially lead to resentment, bitterness, and a massive lightning strike. While Mr. Soon-to-Be Daddy is thinking about the nice summer day and the cold beverage he's enjoying, Ms. Soon-to-Be Mommy is trying to hold down the Saltine she just nibbled on and thinking "hypothetically" of ways to kill him and successfully elude the authorities.

In this case, to make matters worse, the term "new lake house" turned out to actually mean "lake house in need of renovation." To our horror, Meredith and I arrived to discover that there was no central air conditioning! I don't know if you've ever been to South Carolina in July, but trust me: the Vietcong wouldn't hide there without AC. All that passed for relief from the excruciating heat was a small window unit that dated back to the invention of electricity. As the day's temperature quickly climbed to the level of Brazilian-rainforest hot, my pregnant wife—already the hottest person in the group—threw herself on that lone excuse for an air conditioner like a virgin sacrifice before an Aztec god. All the while she kept shooting me "I will kill you and dance on your grave" glances as sweat poured from her baby-carrying body.

Finally, I got the hint that it was my job to correct this problem. Convinced that my wife would burst into flames if we stayed one minute longer, it finally occurred to me to take Meredith to my aunt's air-conditioned home a few miles away. Only, before we left, Meredith somehow managed to sit on a bee. Seconds away from heat stroke and severely bee-stung, my wife limped away from that lake house like a survivor of the Bataan Death March. Safe to say, I can't point to hormones as the only thing that provoked Meredith's inner cat that day. Sure, her hormones may have made her more prone to pounce, but my insensitivity and slowness to act was like prancing through the tiger's den in raw-meat underwear and yelling "Here, kitty kitty!" at the top of my lungs.

The bottom line is, we men need to do more to be aware of how tough it is for you gals to handle all the bodily changes and raging hormones you're dealing with. All I can say is, we'll try to do better. Just know that it's a tough gig for us too—not as tough as what you're going through, but still no walk in the park. So please, don't kill your caveman. Trust me, you'll be sorry if you do. Very soon, you're going to want him around to help change a few thousand diapers.

Chapter 5:
Cavemen in Baby College

As young dads, we sometimes have difficulty figuring out our new roles during pregnancy. Some guys have a strong personality and normally take on the role of leader in a relationship. Maybe their wives defer to their judgment when it comes to many decisions, such as finances, weekend plans, schedules, and so on. Other guys are more laid back. They're content to let their women be the primary decision makers when it comes to the household. Regardless of the dynamic that existed before pregnancy, it's a whole new ballgame once women know they are going to have a baby. Even the most passive of females tend to become more assertive once they're expecting. You mommies have in mind what you want and how you expect things to go when it comes to your soon-to-arrive baby. As expectant fathers, your cavemen have to figure out that it's their job to make your wishes a reality.

The Pregnancy Ninja

Many first-time moms are like my wife, Meredith. When she was pregnant with our first child (my daughter Emerson), Meredith researched everything. She read the magazines, surfed the Internet, and interrogated her doctor relentlessly for information. She had pregnancy down to a system. She steered clear of coffee. Despite loving her evening glass of wine, not a drop passed her lips. She ate the healthiest foods, made sure we registered for the best baby products, bought the safest car seats, and acquired the right glider (which, I had to learn, was a fancy kind of rocker). Meredith was a pregnancy Ninja—well trained and focused! As for me, I was along for the ride. She was Batman, I was Robin. She was Dr. Frankenstein, I was Igor. She was the Jedi knight, I was that annoying frog-like guy that everyone hated in *Star Wars: Episode I—The Phantom Menace*. You get the picture. The point is, with no other kids and nothing outside of work to focus on except our soon-to-be firstborn, my wife was prepared— at least as much as possible.

I kind of enjoyed it. I liked feeling that we were on top of things. I liked even more the fact that Meredith was content to do all of the studying. I just did as I was told. I put the crib together, loaded the glider into a truck, bought the vitamins she needed, drove her to her doctor appointments, and listened when she read excerpts from her pregnancy books out loud. I basically did what a first-time pregnancy husband is supposed to do: be supportive and follow directions.

Welcome to Baby College

Eventually, however, Meredith expected me to become a student as well. In fact, being married to Meredith while she was pregnant was a lot like being in baby college. She inundated me with information. She shared every article, every statistic. More than that, she made me take classes. After all, one can't get caught unprepared. These days, one shouldn't even think of wandering into a delivery room on the big day without having taken several hours of birthing classes and knowing the proper methods for breathing.

Meredith even made me take a pre-delivery-day tour of the hospital. I'd always assumed they'd show us where to go when we arrived to have the baby. Meredith convinced me, however, that we needed to know our way around beforehand. Noting every entrance, exit, hallway, and route from the parking deck to the maternity ward entrance, Meredith studied and planned like a CIA operative plotting to infiltrate an al-Qaeda sleeper cell. According to my wife, all this training was essential. After all, as a husband, how can you expect to have a healthy baby if, during her labor, you accidently tell your wife to breath out when she should have breathed in or have no idea where the maternity ward is in relation to the hospital gift shop?

I'm a Sweathog

Meredith also made me watch instructional DVDs. She had me watch videos of babies being born, babies being changed, babies being burped, and babies being rocked to sleep. I learned that there is a method for everything. One video Meredith made me watch pertained to "soothing your baby." The DVD was put out by some doctor who looked like Gabe Kaplan from *Welcome Back, Kotter*. (Perhaps I'm dating myself by referring to *Welcome Back, Kotter*, but whenever I see a white guy with an Afro and a mustache, I immediately think of that show.) This doctor claimed his method would quiet crying babies and help them fall asleep. *Great,* I thought, *the leader of the Sweathogs* (Mr. Kotter's intellectually challenged students) *is going to teach me how to put my baby to sleep.*

The video featured several couples and their wailing infants. The doctor proceeded to take each baby in his hands, one at a time, and turn it on its side. Mr. Kotter then gently shook each infant while making a shushing sound in his or her ear. He explained that the sound reminded the baby of the noise he or she heard while still inside the mother's womb. At the same time, the motion simulated the movements the baby had grown accustomed to inside of Mommy's uterus. Sure enough, Mr. Kotter's method worked—at least on film.

I never tried the approach on my first child, but I remembered it and gave it a shot with my second. Not long after my son, William, arrived, I realized that I seriously needed a "soothe that child so we can all get some sleep" strategy. I can still remember one night in my son's room. William was going ballistic. About what, I'm not sure. He wasn't sick. He wasn't hungry. He was just mad. He was crying, screaming, and flailing relentlessly. Entering his nursery, I fully expected to find the crib levitating and William's head spinning all the way around on his shoulders. Fortunately, I was relieved to discover no solid signs of demon possession other than his diabolical tantrum. Being a caring father, I picked up my son and attempted to comfort him. I tried talking to him. I tried singing him a song. Nothing worked. His screams became more frustrated. His cries got louder. Then I remembered Mr. Kotter. *Aha!* I thought. *Thank goodness I watched that video!* I turned William on his side, began to jostle him the way I'd seen the doctor do on the DVD, and leaned over to make the calming shushing sound in his ear.

Well, as it turned out, William hadn't seen the video. The shaking only made him madder, and when I leaned in to shush, he kicked me right in the nose with his left foot. Still, I didn't give up. After all, this had to work; I'd seen it in a video. I kept shaking, kept shushing. William got angrier and angrier. His screams filled the entire house. *Must not be shaking enough*, I thought, so I jostled a bit more. *Need to shush louder so he can hear my soothing voice over the crying*, I reasoned, so I turned up the volume on the shushing. Still, it didn't work. Finally, my wife couldn't take it anymore. She pulled herself out of bed (already having been up countless times to nurse the child) and made her way into the room. She entered to find me sitting on the footrest of the glider in my underwear, shaking my son like a Magic Eight Ball, and shushing frantically until saliva hung from my chin like an overheated St. Bernard's. Fearing for the safety of her child, my wife stepped in and took over.

So much for Mr. Kotter's advice. I never tried that method again. Mr. Kotter's approach might work for some people, but it sure didn't work for me. Come to think of it, if I remember the TV show correctly, the Sweathogs weren't too bright. They just couldn't get what Mr. Kotter was trying to teach them. I guess when it comes to baby soothing, I'm pretty much just a Sweathog.

Breastfeeding for Couples

I'll freely admit that I'm not the most sensitive creature on God's earth. I can be selfish and rude without even realizing it. I acknowledge the fact that my wife is a special woman for putting up with me. That said, I think I approached parenthood with the attitude that I wanted to do my part. I wanted to be involved. I knew and willingly embraced the fact that my role would go far beyond passing out cigars on delivery day and playing a few games of catch in the backyard. I wanted to spend time with my kid. I was ready to change the diapers, help with the baths, sing the lullabies, and tackle all the other responsibilities that come with being a parent. There was one area, however, that I assumed my wife would venture into alone: breastfeeding.

Breastfeeding, after all, is a matter of biology. It doesn't matter how much a dad might want to help; there are certain things he just can't do. Last time I checked, feeding a baby milk from one's breast is a duty that clearly falls into the "mommies only" category. Moms breastfeed. Dads don't. Dads can't. Thus, I have to admit that I was somewhat surprised when my wife came home one day and informed me that she had enrolled us in a class entitled Breastfeeding for Couples.

According to my wife, this class was absolutely necessary if she was to have any chance of successfully nursing our child. Apparently, if I didn't sit through five weeks of breastfeeding lectures, Meredith's breasts would shut down, our child would be unable to find her nipples, and life as we know it would cease to exist. Of course, I could have said "no" to the class, but that would have led to a barrage of lightning strikes. Just the fact that I asked the question "Why do I need to go to a class on breastfeeding?" dropped me in the middle of a minefield that I managed to exit only after taking some serious shrapnel.

And so, I went. Every Tuesday night, Meredith and I, along with four or five other couples, took our seats around an oval table at the hospital. We'd sit there and listen while a breastfeeding guru talked to us about breasts, breast milk, breast pumps, breast massages, and breast pads. She showed us charts and videos. She even had a plastic boob that she kept at the end of the table. Personally, I found the boob distracting. Even if I wanted to learn about breastfeeding, I couldn't. Most of the time, I saw the guru's mouth moving, but all I could hear was a little voice inside my head saying, "There's a plastic boob staring at me from the end of this table."

On one occasion, the guru made us pass it around, each taking a turn examining the plastic boob. The women studied it intently. They squeezed it, pondered it, and discussed it. We men, on the other hand, didn't know what to do. It was a plastic boob, for gosh sakes! When it came to me, I wasn't sure how to handle it. Hold it too long and I'd look like a pervert. Don't hold it long enough and I'd look like I'm trying to hide the fact that I'm a pervert. When it finally reached me, I reluctantly took it. I could feel the beads of sweat forming on my forehead. All eyes were on me. All I could think was, *My wife is sitting next to me, watching me fondle a plastic boob.* Then, out of nowhere, the guru blindsided me with a question: "Kindred, can you find the milk ducts?" *Milk ducts? What the heck are milk ducts?* I'm sure the guru had told us, but again, I was entranced by the plastic boob and heard nothing. To me, milk ducts sounded like something a cheap neighbor gives kids at Halloween because he didn't want to spend the extra money on M&Ms. No, I couldn't find the milk ducts! And I wasn't about to run my hand over the plastic boob looking for them.

The women loved the class. With pens and paper in hand, they took meticulous notes. They asked tons of questions, each time scribbling frantically as the guru explained where the baby's mouth should be, how a mom should hold her child, or what to do if the baby wouldn't latch on correctly. Like a devoted platoon of pre-lactating commandos, these gals were focused and ready for their mission. They were going to breastfeed, doggone it! And God help anyone who tried to keep them from shoving milk-spouting nipples into their babies' hungry mouths!

The men had a somewhat different experience. Sometimes, I'd look around the room at the expressions on the other soon-to-be-dads' faces. Like me, they were just staring into the distance, unable to feel—numb from the experience. Their mouths said nothing, but their eyes and faces screamed, "Kill me! Kill me now!" While other guys were out grabbing a beer or catching a ballgame, we were watching the guru caress the plastic boob and listening as she used words like *engorged*. We had no dignity left. Every ounce of manhood had been stripped away. As a man, you can't be a part of any gathering with the word *breastfeeding* in the title and still feel your testicles. Nope, we left our testosterone at the door. There we sat, week in and week out, dutiful eunuchs accompanying our wives and paying homage to the plastic boob.

For five weeks, the plastic boob commanded our devotion like a pagan idol. The guru was its high priestess, our wives her faithful disciples. As for us dads, all we wanted to do was get home as quickly as possible after each class. While our wives talked, laughed, exchanged numbers, and genuinely got to know each other, we guys occasionally shook hands and exchanged small talk, but only because we couldn't get our wives to the car fast enough. As the women compared pregnancy experiences, the men looked at one another as if to say, "Hey, man, I won't tell anyone I saw you here if you don't tell anyone you saw me."

There were times I thought of rebelling. But with a pregnant wife, you pick your battles. Some things are worth getting pounced on by the hormonal tiger, others aren't. In the end, I reasoned that cutting breastfeeding class wasn't worth the bite marks. Besides, some of the guru's input was good. She talked to us husbands about getting up to change the baby's diapers so that Mommy won't have to. She pointed out how important it will be for us dads to protect Mommy's sleep time because she's going to be exhausted from feeding the baby every two hours. Basically, the message was simple: don't be a selfish jackass! Get up and help! Right. Got it. But did I really need the guru to tell me that? Couldn't my wife have told me just as easily? In fact, hasn't she gotten pretty good at pointing out to me when I'm being a selfish jackass? Maybe my wife feared I wouldn't listen if I only heard it from her. Perhaps that's why she felt she needed to bring in the guru.

In the end, the real value in my going to the class was that it made my wife feel supported. She thought it was important, so that made it worthwhile. I guess you could also argue that the class worked. My wife has successfully breastfed three children. (Our two youngest were adopted when they were seven months old, so they were both bottle fed.) As for me, I'm still working on the "don't be a selfish jackass" part. Guess I'm not as fast a learner as Meredith.

Unintentional Jackassedness

Speaking of selfish jackasses, maybe there are times when you wonder if your caveman is one because he doesn't seem as enthusiastic about all the researching and class-taking as you do. My guess is that he's not trying to be unsupportive. Any jackassedness on his part is most likely unintentional. It's just that baby college is a bit uncomfortable for us guys. Not that actual college wasn't hard too, but at least then we got to go to frat parties and football games.

We men want to be supportive; we just don't get the reasoning behind all of the baby prep. We don't see the same need for it that women do. As we figure it, early Native Americans and the first pioneers didn't take Lamaze classes, yet they had babies just fine. Our great-grandparents never watched a birthing video, and many of them had more than ten kids. Childbirth is arguably the most natural process in the history of humankind. The baby is going to come. A couple of contractions into it, Mommy will figure out how to push. Sure, there can be complications. But covering complications isn't what these birthing classes are for. The doctor is going to handle any problems regardless of whether you've taken your baby prep courses or not. Still, for some reason most cavemen can't grasp, women want us to watch the videos, take the classes, and train with other couples. Not that we men mind meeting other expecting couples, it's just that it's a little awkward asking another guy what he does for a living while his wife is lying three feet away with her legs spread apart, practicing delivery-day breathing techniques.

Yes, most cavemen will go to baby college if you want them to. I've known very few who won't. That's because we recognize that it's a big deal to you, the new mommies that we love. Most cavemen reason that the least we can do is go to the classes, watch the DVDs, and, if called upon to do so, even handle a plastic boob. Just know that if we seem less than enthusiastic it's not because we're meaning to be selfish jackasses. It just means we find it a little uncomfortable and, quite often, bewildering.

Chapter 6:
A New Set of Rocks

If guys are cavemen, then pregnancy is a whole new cave. It's a new habitat to which men must adjust. The carvings on the stone walls aren't the same. The boulders are all in different places.

Why is this a big deal? Simple: cavemen are creatures of habit. We like our routine. Don't forget, we want to control things and know what we're dealing with. (Not that we ever do, but it's nice when we can live under the delusion that we're on top of things.) It's hard enough figuring out how to navigate the relationship and marriage caves. Just when we think we're beginning to know our way around those tricky environments, pregnancy comes along and moves all the rocks again.

Caveman Opinions; They Mean Nothing

As a soon-to-be dad, I had to learn that one of my most important jobs was to have an opinion about everything, but that

I shouldn't make the mistake of thinking that my opinion about anything actually mattered. If Meredith asked me what color I thought the baby's room should be or which crib sheets I liked best, I needed to have an answer. Failure to do so would communicate to her that I didn't care enough about our baby. In reality, I had no preference regarding what color we painted the nursery. My only condition was that it wouldn't be pink if the baby was a boy. Not to be homophobic, but I didn't want my son sleeping in a pink room. I'm sure, in the long run, it wouldn't have mattered. It's just a color. But if years later I had ever come home to catch my son trying on his mother's clothes and blasting "It's Raining Men" over the loud-speakers, I know I would have thought back to that pink room and wondered, *What if ...?*

The point is, a caveman has to learn that answers like, "Honey, it doesn't matter to me; just pick the one you like," simply doesn't cut it. I know because, early on, I tried such responses. I sincerely didn't care how we decorated the baby's room, what fabric Meredith chose for the glider, what brand of highchair we registered for, or whether we placed the crib against the short wall or the long one. Like most expecting daddies, I thought that by saying it didn't matter I was communicating to my wife that I trusted her judgment. What I eventually figured out was that she interpreted my lack of an opinion as a sign that I didn't care about our soon-to-be-born child. Of course, nothing could have been further from the truth! Still, "I don't care" is what Meredith heard. So, after a few hurt feelings, a couple of fights I never saw coming, and several scorching lightning strikes, I learned to have opinions.

I learned just as quickly, however, that my opinions really didn't matter. My wife already knew what she wanted, and she was not about to be deterred by what I thought. Once all this finally sunk into my Neanderthal brain, life got a little easier. Our conversations normally went something like this:

> Meredith: "Honey, should we put the glider in the corner or against the wall?"
> Kindred: "I think it looks better against the wall."
> Meredith: "Really? I think I want it in the corner."

> Meredith: "Honey, do you like the white highchair or the one with patterns?"
> Kindred: "I vote for white."
> Meredith: "I think we'll take the one with patterns."

> Meredith: "Honey, which maternity shirt should I buy?"
> Kindred: "The one on the left, definitely."
> Meredith: "Hmm. I really like the one on the right."

And so the game is played. Expecting dads should learn to have opinions. Failing to do so will hurt a pregnant mommy's feelings and lead to a lot of 3:00 a.m. apology sessions. On the other hand, cavemen shouldn't make the mistake of expecting their opinions to mean anything. Let's face it, you women don't need our opinions in order to make a decision. You just want to know that we dads are engaged in the whole planning-for-baby process.

Opinions or Not, Your Caveman Cares

Of course, until men learn the true intent behind a woman's questions, great potential for frustration and conflict abounds. To a woman, a man voicing his opinion about some baby-related detail is interpreted as a gesture of love and support. To a man, expressing a preference about something a woman has already decided seems like a waste of time and an exercise in insanity. The way men figure it, there's no sense in voicing an opinion when you know your significant other has already made up her mind. As a result, pregnancies (especially first pregnancies) can feature more than their share of arguments over baby planning. A woman is likely to get offended by the fact that her caveman can't form a strong opinion about nursery designs or stroller sizes. Her man, in turn, gets frustrated and defensive when grilled with questions about baby details he hasn't even pondered. He can't understand how his wife equates his failure to favor one pattern of crib sheets over another to a lack of caring. Meanwhile, his wife can't fathom how a loving soon-to-be father could possibly fail to prefer one brand of Pack 'n Play over another. And round and round we go.

Don't worry, young mommies; men eventually catch on to the fact that they need to have opinions, especially if they've been married for any length of time and this is not their wife's first pregnancy. Until they do, just know that failure to have opinions about baby décor or onesies *DOES NOT* mean your cavemen don't care. They honestly think you have a better opinion regarding how to get the nursery ready or what baby supplies to load up on. They totally trust you with those decisions.

Your cavemen are thinking about the baby too. They're just concerned with different things. They're busy thinking about how to plan for the baby's future and afford all the additional expenses that come with parenthood. Expecting mommies tend to think about the baby's immediate needs and comfort. Expecting daddies tend to think about the baby's long-term needs and security. Am I generalizing? Sure. But I've found that these patterns commonly emerge. Men and women tend to have different priorities when it comes to preparing for a baby. That's okay. No one is right or wrong. After all, babies have short-term, immediate needs that must be met, and it is wise to plan responsibly for a child's future. The encouraging thing for moms to remember is that men, just like women, think they are focusing on what's most important for the baby's welfare and are striving to make sure their child is well taken care of.

Some Assembly Required

One of the things new dads must do is learn to assemble things. For some men, this is a piece of cake. Then there are guys like me; I'm no handyman. I take on building projects as a matter of necessity only. I find that my blood pressure, temptation to use profanity, likelihood of throwing things, and tendency to threaten inanimate objects as if they were living beings, all increase significantly when I try to put things together. As dads, however, men have little choice. Unless they've got enough money to buy everything pre-assembled or hire folks to do it for them, new fathers quickly learn that it's build or perish.

My first assembly task involved furniture for the baby's room. I consider myself a relatively strong Christian, but few things war against a man's righteousness more than a thousand "some assembly required" pieces of baby furniture and a set of directions that hardly make sense. After about twenty minutes of trying to put together my first child's crib, I realized that curse words were beginning to fill my mind. They started small—a few d-words; a couple of references to the devil's eternal stomping grounds. As time wore on, however, and my frustration increased, I noticed that the bad words weren't just in my mind anymore; they were actually coming out of my mouth.

Three hours later, there I was, standing over a half-assembled crib and holding a mobile of little lambs and smiling stars in one hand and a Phillips screw driver in the other. As my last ounces of sanity ebbed, I heard myself yelling things like:

- "How come this *bleepin'* screw doesn't look like the one in the *bleepin'* picture!"

- "Why is the *bleepin'* smiley moon facing outward? The *bleepin'* smiley moon should face inward!"

- "Where's the piece with the *bleepin'* happy cow? The directions say there should be a *bleepin'* happy cow!"

Finally, Meredith came waltzing in with her customary bowl of popcorn to find me crouched in the corner and up to my knees in faux wood and bolts. There I sat, like Jack Nicholson in *The Shining*, sweating profusely and pulling at my disheveled hair. Blankly I stared into the abyss, drool running down my chin as the words "all work and no play makes Jack a dull boy" ran over and over again through my tortured mind. Then, with a casual tone that, to me, sounded mockingly cruel, my wife asked, "Didn't you look at the instructions?"

For a second, the next day's headlines flashed before my eyes: "Lunatic Husband Attacks Wife after Heartless Crib Taunt." Remembering, however, that I deeply love my wife and that any aggressive move on my part might unleash the hormonal tiger, I managed to restrain myself and, instead, simply lost it. Rising to my feet, I unleashed what I'm sure was an inexcusable tirade of unintelligible babble. I think I even threw a few pieces of the crib (not at Meredith). When it was over, I sank back to the floor exhausted. Defeated by the crib and humbled by the futility of my efforts, all I could do was sit there panting, hoping that my health insurance would cover at least one week's stay in a mental institution.

A little while later, after the demons had gone and I had regained some of my composure (regaining my dignity would have been too much to ask), my wife and I finally assembled the crib together. Ten "easy steps" completed in just under five hours and one massive emotional meltdown. To this day, I still don't know what all those extra crib pieces were for. But five babies later, that crib's still going strong; no little Howards have ever fallen through it. So, as far as I'm concerned, we're good.

Pray for Patience, Proceed with Caution

I'd like to say that the crib was a one-time deal. Unfortunately, it has been a pattern too often repeated. Chest of drawers, changing tables, beds, bikes, sticker-making machines, princess palaces, and most recently a basketball goal have all bested me, leaving my manhood dashed and scattered on the rocks of "some assembly required." The only advice I can offer is this: if your caveman is like me, not a natural builder and assembler, pray God gives him patience and the ability to grasp directions! He's gonna need it. With fatherhood comes a lot of assembling. Some days it's not so bad. I manage to surprise myself by putting something together with only limited problems. Even more astonishing, I sometimes stay patient and calm despite major difficulties. Most of the time, I let my wife assemble things. It might not be manly, but she's better at it and more patient than I am. She completes projects without throwing tools or threatening to hunt down and kill the manufacturer. Once in a while, I take on an assemble-it-yourself task. Those are the nights I usually end up sitting on the garage floor, rubbing my temples repeatedly, and striving in vain to go to my "happy place."

Pray that God also gives you patience—*with your caveman.* There's a good chance that, unlike me, he'll refuse to surrender and insist on remaining the ordained assembler of the family, even if you're better at it than he is. Why? It's a man thing. Our frustration doesn't stem from the fact that the crib or changing table we just spent six hours trying to build falls apart, as much as it does from the feeling that we've failed. We want to be successful at whatever task we take on because we view ourselves as doing it for you and our baby! You're carrying the kid, after all. We want to provide you with whatever you need, even if it means building something. To us, it's not just about putting the safety gates up; it's about being what you and our baby need. We don't want to fail or let you down.

Sound silly? Maybe. But didn't you cry the first time you tried to make dinner as a young wife and every smoke alarm in the house went off? So I'd encourage you to hang in there with your caveman. Some cavemen turn out to be pretty good assemblers. In fact, I would dare say that most will (I am one of the sad exceptions). Regardless, just tread lightly if you feel your caveman would be better off leaving the assembling to someone else. To him, it may not be simply an issue of putting things together; it may also be a matter of male pride.

Let Him Finish

Oh, and if you see your caveman losing his temper or attempting to strangle a piece of assemble-it-yourself baby furniture, don't get too discouraged. He'll be fine once the project is over and he's had a half hour or so to decompress. That's just how he works through things. I'm not saying that it's right. In fact, I think men should make a conscious effort to control their tempers. The Bible even commands as much. I'm just saying that many men occasionally succumb to the "some assembly required" induced fit. Right or wrong, it happens.

What might help a woman is to truly understand what is actually going on. What, to a woman, looks like an insane rant and a reason to keep a therapist on speed dial is, to a man, simply a method of self-help therapy. Sure, you might want to talk to your caveman once he's calmed down and explain to him why you wish he would remain calm or express himself differently; after all, we're not talking about continually ignoring or condoning bad behavior here. But my advice would be to use discretion when considering whether or not to approach him while he's in the throngs of his emotional outburst. If you're not careful, you'll actually throw gasoline on the fire. Even if you're right and your points make sense, he won't be in an emotional place where he can hear them. He's lost it (temporarily). The thin thread by which he's been hanging is unraveling, and one comment from you could be the scissors that totally sever it, dropping him into the pit of mental breakdown. My advice? As long as he's not going nuts in front of the kids or posing a danger to anyone, let him finish. Remember, it's not actually as bad as you think. It's just him thinking out loud. Once he's done and has regained some semblance of control, then you can have a constructive talk about his behavior.

To reiterate, I'm not saying you should accept your caveman's fits of rage or his outbursts of profanity; I'm just saying be wise about when you decide to broach the subject. Otherwise, what would have been a thirty minute tirade aimed at a bassinet may instead turn into a marital argument featuring comments both parties regret and a day of not speaking to one another.

It's All about the Family

Some roles are filled easier by certain dads than others. Certain dads are great assemblers, but they lack the patience and sensitivity to sit through Breastfeeding for Couples or attend birthing classes without their misery being evident. Other men are more considerate but can't assemble a piece of furniture or put up safety gates without having to file some sort of insurance claim before it's over. Regardless of what camp your caveman falls into, it's important to remember that most soon-to-be fathers want to fulfill all the traditional "daddy roles."

What your caveman might need help understanding is this: what he does is often as much about attitude as it is about performance. He sometimes forgets that his wife isn't just looking for him to do the right thing; she needs to perceive that he's doing the right thing because he *wants to*, not because he has to. You'd think we cavemen would already know this. But, for some guys, you're going to have to spell it out.

Sure, some of the things we do as expectant fathers aren't fun. Of course, we'd rather watch the game, get some work done, hit the golf course, or go on a date with our wives instead of listening to pregnancy facts or weighing the convenience of disposable diapers against the environmental friendliness of cloth ones. But, as men, most of us try to remember that it's not about us; it's about you—our wives and soon-to-be mothers of our babies.

Chapter 7:
Cavemen on D-Day

Despite all our down-to-the-detail planning and total preparedness, Meredith's due date with our first child came and went. Nearly a week after our daughter was supposed to be born, there still was no baby.

I wasn't overly concerned. My thought was that we just keep doing what we were doing. Get up, live life, take care of the normal daily business; the baby will get here when she gets here. Meredith, however, had other plans. She was tired of carrying a baby for nine months. Like a college dropout living in his parents' basement and playing video games, it was time for this kid to get out. Meredith went on offense. She'd done her research, and she had a few tricks up her sleeve to speed up the process.

Twister, Anyone?

As a husband, one has to be supportive of his pregnant wife's labor-inducing efforts, even if he initially doesn't see the need for them. To me, it seemed that the wise thing to do was just wait. Don't do anything. Sit tight and let nature take its course. The baby will come when she wants. If she is three weeks late, so what? All that matters is that she be born healthy, right?

Easy for us guys to say. We're not the ones who've been carrying the kid in our bodies for nine months. It's not our bladder the child's been doing jumping jacks on. We aren't the ones carrying enough water to irrigate half of Sudan. No, we just need to concede that a pregnant woman has legitimate reasons for wanting to induce labor. Unfortunately, we men often don't understand this right off the bat. In fact, most men are shocked to learn that they or their young mommies have any say about when the baby comes. Women like my wife, however, have educated themselves. They know that there are options. They're aware of things a couple can do to encourage a delivery.

To my surprise, sex is one of the things that supposedly induces labor. I'm not sure how. Whatever the reason, sex is supposed to work. Thus, once Meredith decided to take labor matters into her own hands, the sexual dynamic in our household changed; Meredith became the primary pursuer.

Of course, sex wasn't exactly the same as it had been a few months earlier. When a woman is nine months pregnant, having sex means being creative. She's still beautiful, but her body has definitely changed. Some of the old approaches just won't work. Having sex nine months into a pregnancy is kind of like playing

Twister for the first time in twenty years. It can still be fun, but not long into the game you realize that you just can't make it to "left hand green" the way you used to. Awkward as it could be at times, we gave it our best shot.

The other thing Meredith said we should do was walk. So we walked. We walked and walked. We walked up and down the street, all around Piedmont Park, and all over Virginia Highlands (our neighborhood in Atlanta). Two nights before we went to the hospital, Meredith thought maybe it was time. She nudged me until I woke up and told me that she was sure she'd go into labor if we could just walk. I suggested sex. She put on her shoes. Since you don't wear shoes to play Twister, I knew I'd been shot down. Not that I really wanted sex either. What I wanted was sleep. But it was almost two in the morning, and I figured that sex would at least mean not having to get out of bed. Unable to dissuade my wife from her labor-inducing endeavors, I rolled out of bed and put on my tennis shoes.

There I was, alongside my wife, walking up and down the road in front of our apartment in the predawn hours, wiping the sleep from my eyes and hoping Meredith would have a contraction. The night was quiet except for our conversation and the sound of a few drunks making their way home from the nearby bars. For close to an hour, we trekked back and forth. Nothing—still no labor. The next day, Meredith made me walk at least two miles around the park, again hoping that it would launch her little body into labor. Sure enough, within twenty-four hours, the time finally came. I don't know if the walking or the Twister sex had anything to do with it, but Meredith at last was about to give birth to our first baby. Shortly before noon on the following day, we headed to the hospital, anxious to meet our daughter face-to-face.

Forget the Script

Expectant moms probably spend more time imagining what their first child's delivery day will be like than dads do. Even so, as a soon-to-be dad anticipating the arrival of my baby, I had an image in my head. After all, we'd trained for this. My wife would know when it was time. I'd drive her to the hospital. After checking in at the desk (smiles on our faces due to the joy of the moment), I'd keep Meredith company while she went through the early stages of labor. As a highly trained delivery coach, I'd remind her how to breathe, help her from her wheelchair to the bed, hold her hand, and basically be Mr. Wonderful. Once in the delivery room, I'd be by her side throughout the entire process. With my skillful coaching and the doctor's medical expertise, Meredith would sail through labor with flying colors. She'd give birth to a beautiful baby girl. We'd look at each other. She'd cry. I'd meet family in the waiting room to announce that our little girl was healthy and gorgeous. It would be an awesome day!

What most expecting parents come to realize is that, while imagination is putting the finishing touches on its perfect plans, reality is often laughing hysterically in the background and thinking, *What an idiot!* If months of birthing classes are like rehearsing for a play, then the actual delivery is opening night. Things rarely go as rehearsed when the auditorium fills with people and the lead actor suddenly forgets a line. Nothing can totally prepare you for the actual delivery. Women roll with the punches. They have to; they're in pain and having a baby. They don't have the luxury of trying to "stick to the plan." Men, however, are planners. All too often, it takes a caveman a little longer to realize that it's okay to deviate from the original script in order to make the show come off successfully.

Mommy Wants Her E-p-i-d-u-r-a-l

When we arrived at the hospital, Meredith and I were met at the registration desk by a woman with all the charm of someone who had just learned she was being audited. She couldn't have cared less that my wife was in labor—everyone she dealt with was in labor. Little Miss Sunshine took my wife's name, and then, with a level of hospitality usually reserved for prison strip searches, proceeded to shove a clipboard of paperwork at us. "Fill these out," she barked.

Meanwhile, all Meredith cared about was not missing her window for anesthesia. My wife had read stories of idealistic moms who had approached their first delivery determined to give birth naturally, without any painkillers. Passing the point of no return, many of them ended up screaming "Drug me!" only to be met with the sad news that it was too late.

Hoping to avoid such a scenario, my wife made sure the hospital staff knew she had no interest in tackling natural childbirth. Her favorite word from the time we arrived at the hospital was *epidural*. Meredith was not the least bit tempted to soak up the "full experience" of the natural birthing process. She figured that God, in His sovereign wisdom, had predestined her to give birth in the age of modern medicine. Determined to abide by His will, Meredith voiced her desire for drugs to anyone who would listen.

> Receptionist: "Name of insurance provider?"
> Meredith: "Epidural."
>
> Nurse: "Can I get you anything?"
> Meredith: "Yes, an epidural."
>
> Doctor: "So, what are you going to name the baby?"
> Meredith: "Epidural."
>
> Administrator: "Please spell your first name for me."
> Meredith: "E-p-i-d-u-r-a-l."

Finally, Meredith got her anesthesia. No doubt about it, when you are about to have another human being rip and pull her way out of your body, an epidural is your best friend.

Perhaps, like Meredith, you've decided to take advantage of medical advancements to avoid as much pain as possible. That's okay. In my opinion, you're not cheating yourself or the baby. My wife didn't experience "natural" childbirth with any of our kids, and they all seem fine. Plus, she experienced more than enough "nature" the nine months leading up to each birth and for roughly a year afterwards as she breastfed.

On the other hand, maybe you're determined to experience birth the old fashioned way. That's great too. Just know that if you change the plan at the hospital, your caveman might be caught off guard. Without question, your decision to switch gears and use some drugs is understandable, but remember that you've probably spent the previous few months preparing for and selling your caveman on the pluses of natural childbirth. Changing course on d-day may go against his prehistoric instincts and initially confuse him. He might wonder if you'll regret your decision later and attempt to talk you out of using pain killers. My point is simply this: if you're pregnant and planning to go natural, you might want to have the "If I change my mind and ask for drugs, make sure you honor my wishes or I'll rip your throat out with my bare hands" conversation before the big day arrives. That way, instead of feeling like he's deviating from a plan, your caveman will know that it's a built-in part of the plan.

Ah, the Waiting

Next came the waiting. From the time Meredith finally got her painkillers to the time our daughter arrived, several hours elapsed. As Meredith dealt with the gradually increasing contractions, I passed the time trying to make her comfortable, calling family members and friends to let them know that the big day had arrived, and watching television. Fortunately, Meredith and I had talked ahead of time and I knew exactly what she expected of me at the hospital. My main job was to help her feel comfortable and stay calm. I probably would have known this instinctively, but, again, given that I'm a caveman, it was wise of Meredith to make sure we were on the same page beforehand.

Meredith ended up feeling more anxious than I had anticipated. Every time the baby moved in Meredith's belly, the hospital monitor would lose our daughter's heartbeat, causing Meredith to worry that something was wrong. I finally stepped up and insisted that the nurses turn off the equipment in the room and simply monitor the baby from their desk. Eventually, Meredith calmed down a bit, but she remained somewhat on edge throughout most of her labor.

A daddy-to-be has to be attentive and sensitive to his wife's needs and anxieties. The expectant dad's job is to be his wife's servant. What she needs, he does his best to provide. Sometimes that means fetching her purse or getting her something to drink. Other times, it may involve being her advocate, such as when I had to insist that the nurses turn off the monitor in Meredith's room. Basically, a daddy has got to be whatever his new mommy needs. If he needs to stand up and insist on something, then he's got to do it. His wife is giving birth. He's her protector and about to be his child's protector too. Fathers don't have the luxury of being timid.

The truth is, men actually do better on delivery day when they are given tasks to complete. We get insecure when we don't know what to do. An expecting father feels he should be doing something for the woman he loves, especially when she's in labor. The problem is that he often doesn't know what. His instincts tell him to do something to take away his new mom's pain, anxiety, and discomfort. But the reality is that there is very little he can do. Sometimes, all he can provide is a hand or arm for his wife to grab onto or a body that she can yell at when the pain and fatigue of labor becomes too much. Just remember, if your husband seems nervous or overly attentive to you to the point that he is getting on your nerves rather than helping, make up something for him to do. Send him to get a cup of water, call a relative, fetch you a book, or retrieve something you left in the car. Not only will it get him to stop bugging you for a few minutes, but it will also allow him to feel in control of something, thereby helping him to relax and probably making him more useful to you later when you really need him.

A Tool for Good or Evil

While most men I know do a pretty good job of taking care of mommy on delivery day, there is one trap into which all men must be careful not to fall. Labor can go on for hours and hours. While waiting with their new mommies for their little bundles of joy to arrive, men must remain on their guard against the seductive powers of the infamous labor room television! As busy adults, it's rare that most men have time to just sit and watch TV. Labor, however, often requires long periods of waiting. Expectant fathers are left sitting with little to do. To pass the time, most young fathers inevitably find themselves watching television.

On the surface it seems innocent enough. After all, that's why the hospital put a TV in the room—to give you something to do while you wait. But dads need to be careful. Like so many things in life, the maternity ward television can be a tool for both good and evil. As guys, if we're not alert, we can all too easily be sucked in by the power of the tube. What begins as casual television viewing meant to kill some time can quickly morph into total immersion into whatever program a man is watching. This can lead to serious trouble. At any moment, a caveman's delivering mommy could call for him to hold her hand through a contraction. If he's not sharp, he might commit the serious offense of responding with comments like, "One second, Honey, I just want to see this play," or "Huh, did you say something?"

Especially if your caveman is a sports fan, the maternity ward television can become an instrument of Satan used to destroy him. If there's a game on and he's not extra careful, he may not even notice your cries for attention over his own shouts of *"No!* What are you doing!" or "Come on, cover the spread!" So warn your caveman about the maternity ward television. As long as he's aware of the danger, he should do a good job of staying on his guard and continually making a conscious effort to remain tuned in to you. Otherwise, if he falls prey to the seductive forces of the television, he's likely to enrage his baby-delivering wife to the point that he ends up with a bedpan on his head or an IV bottle imbedded in his backside. Either way, he'll probably stop watching television.

One Caveman's Delivery Story

After several hours of labor, Meredith's doctor made the judgment call that our first child needed to be delivered via a C-section. Shortly before midnight, the nursing staff maneuvered my wife out of her labor room and down the hall for surgery.

Meanwhile, I was handed a suit that looked like something worn by members of a hazmat team confronting a chemical leak. It covered me from head to foot, only allowing a slit for my eyes and openings for my hands. It even had covers for my feet. The whole outfit was disposable and made of paper. Second only to the knit tie and pointed dress shoes I'd donned for my eighth-grade dance, it was the dorkiest outfit I've ever worn. I could hear the few cool points I'd accumulated in my life falling to the floor and breaking as I shuffled from the labor room to the OR. The worst part was having to stand in the hallway by myself, fully decked out in my paper attire, while everyone who knew who I was entered the operating room to prepare my wife for surgery. As nurses and doctors passed me in the hall, I imagined them thinking, "Who's the geek in the napkin ensemble?" Everything in me wanted to announce:

> "Hello. No, I'm not a pathetic loser. I don't dress like a surgeon and hang out at hospitals trying to meet girls. I don't live with my mother and collect Star Wars action figures. I'm actually an expectant dad. I was told to wear this. I was told to wait here. No, really, I'm not lying. I actually look cool sometimes; not right now, mind you, but sometimes."

At last, Meredith's nurse stepped out to rescue me from my nerdish limbo. I entered the room to find Meredith lying on the table and prepped for her operation. She was fully awake, although the epidural meant that she could feel nothing from her chest down. A curtain-like sheet shielded her from any view of the procedure that was about to take place. I, on the other hand, was able to see everything. At one point, I looked over the curtain just in time to see my little girl's head sitting on top of Meredith's belly. She was facing me, eyes closed, her head shaped like a football and covered in goo. She wasn't completely quiet, but she wasn't really crying yet either. God only knows what was going through her little mind. Whatever it was, I'm sure it was a newborn's equivalent of "What the hell?!"

The whole process was incredible! After it was over, the nurses took my daughter, cut the umbilical cord, and cleaned her up. Then, in a moment I'll never forget, they brought my baby girl to me. "Mr. Howard, meet your daughter," the nurse said. I was all smiles under that paper mask. I had the honor of being the one to show my little girl to my wife for the first time. I knelt next to Meredith as the same doctors who'd operated on her now worked diligently to tend to her wounds. Meredith was an emotional whirlwind. She was ecstatic to see her daughter. She was exhausted from the hours of labor and brief surgery. She was sad that she didn't get the chance to deliver vaginally and couldn't hold her baby right away. As most mothers would at such a moment, Meredith began to cry. Through her tears, my wife smiled at our daughter and stammered, "She's gorgeous." Meredith was right; she was.

Do "Heads Ups" Ahead of Time

I believe most men want to be Mr. Wonderful on delivery day. But, as with so many other things, some good talks ahead of time can help make sure your caveman knows what you need and expect from him when the big day arrives. You also might want to assure him in advance that whatever names you call him (or the mother who gave birth to him) while you're in the throngs of birthing pains are not necessarily a true reflection of how you feel and should not be taken personally.

In the end, delivery is a physically exhausting day for mommies and an insecure place for cavemen. Trust me, things won't go as expected. But as long as mommy and baby are healthy, that's okay. One day, the challenges and unexpected turns will make for your sweetest and most hilarious delivery-day stories.

SECTION III:

The Baby Cave

Chapter 8:
Your Temporary Home

Following your baby's birth, the hospital maternity ward becomes a new parent's temporary home. For all couples, their time there turns out to be an experience they'll never forget. Yes, it is memorable because it is the joyous first few days of your baby's life. But it is also a training ground, at least for first-time parents. It's where you and your spouse jump off the safe cliff of parenting theory into the raging rapids of parental reality. No more plastic boobs or diaper changing classes. Now real breastfeeding and actual poop cleaning are demanded.

At least in the maternity ward, you're not alone. There are nurses and baby experts standing by to help if you need them. For a few days you can return the child to the safety of the hospital nursery whenever you desperately need some sleep. But still, it's a different world. You know the clock is ticking. Before long, the hospital will take the training wheels off and send you home to fend for yourselves. Then, it's just the two of you and a little person who is totally dependent on you to meet his or her every need. No pressure.

Not Made for Fathers

As dads, few places on earth are more perplexing than a maternity ward. When my siblings and I were born, dads remained in the waiting room, anxiously waiting to hear whether they needed to run out and buy a baseball glove or a baby doll. Today's generation of dads is expected to be much more involved (and rightfully so).

If you're a mom who is about to have her first baby—or if you have someone you trust who can watch your older children— your caveman will likely stay with you in your maternity ward room. While this is a good thing, allowing Dad to better serve his new mommy, meet her needs, and maximize time with his new child, it can also be a bit uncomfortable for many dads. That's because maternity wards aren't made for fathers. They're made for mothers. Dads are an afterthought. Like disoriented Neanderthals who just got stomped on by a mastodon, daddies find themselves dazed and confused. They're insecure and lost in a strange land of breast pumps, plastic nipples, and people with titles like Lactation Specialist.

If your caveman spends the night in your room, then chances are good that he will be forced to sleep in a fetal position on a bed the size of which suggests it was made for someone named Grumpy, Sneezy, or Doc. If he was irresponsible and didn't attend Breastfeeding for Couples, he is likely to be caught by surprise and feel weak and helpless when his wife experiences physical pain or emotional distress caused by breastfeeding difficulties. And, because the hospital doesn't feed him, he's liable to need an intestinal transplant after two or three days of feasting at the hospital's onsite fast-food restaurant. Add to all this the fact that he is expected to navigate this strange, maternal land as his wife's servant, advocate, and occasional runner, and you've got a real recipe for feelings of inadequacy. I've seen men who run businesses, oversee million dollar projects, and/or are paid six-figure salaries to solve major problems come totally unglued and look like buffoons trying to make their way around a maternity ward. To this day, I still bear the scar of a second-degree burn suffered while trying to reheat a bowl of hospital-issued grits. For men who like to fix things and be in control, a maternity ward can be a humbling place to hang out.

The Curious Case of Meredith Howard

Following our oldest child's birth, Meredith developed a mysterious fever. For two weeks, the doctors couldn't figure out why Meredith's temperature would not return to normal. Baffled, the doctors insisted that we could not go home while Meredith's temperature was above ninety-nine degrees.

This brings me to a common caveman pet peeve about hospitals. Following a birth, doctors and nurses keep telling Mommy to get rest. Then, these same medical professionals proceed to enter her room every half hour to take her temperature, check her bandages, or generally just bug the heck out of her all night long. It's amazing the amount of information that these Florence Nightingales just "have" to know at one o'clock in the morning. They "needed" my wife's blood, a urine sample, her blood pressure, her horoscope, her autograph, her license plate number, her grandmother's casserole recipe, the name of her favorite contestant on *American Idol* ... anything to keep her from sleeping! Just a heads up to any medical professionals reading this: if a mom who's just given birth or had a C-section needs rest, try staying out of her room so she can actually get some—especially if she's got an unexplained fever!

Despite the late-night interruptions, Meredith eventually felt better after a few days. Still, the nurses with the midnight temperature checks kept telling us that she had a fever. A vicious cycle evolved. Meredith would feel fine; we'd think we were taking our baby home, and then a doctor would look at her chart and tell us it would be one more day. Feel fine, high temperature, doctor insists on one more day. For two weeks, this trend continued. Meredith and I began to wonder if we would ever get out of the hospital. I could just see us making the tabloid headlines: "Baby

Raised in Maternity Ward!" Maybe we'd even get our own reality TV show. It appeared we were well on our way to being famous.

Meanwhile, my daughter, Emerson, began to look freakishly big next to the other newborns in the hospital. Babies grow at a rapid rate. Most of the kids in the nursery were in and out of there in two to four days. Emerson, however, was beginning to look like a lifer at the state pen. All her pals were serving their sentence and then getting out. She, on the other hand, was left behind to do hard time. Once, as I was returning her to the hospital nursery, I could swear I heard her refer to the place as "The Rock." By the time she finally made it out of there, my daughter was running the joint. When Emerson yelled "Poop!" the other babies asked "How much?" A couple of times, I think the nurses even caught some of the other infants sneaking my daughter pacifiers in exchange for protection from the other inmates.

Finally, after two weeks in a holding pattern, we made it out. By that time, every specialist short of a horticulturalist and an expert in animal husbandry had seen my wife. Another day or two, and I'm sure they would have given their two cents' worth as well. The doctors finally concluded that my wife was fine and that it might actually be all the antibiotics they were giving her that were causing the fever. Resisting the impulse to jump across my wife's bed and strangle the doctor who delivered that enlightening news, I instead focused on the exciting revelation that we were free to go and threw all my frustrated energy into packing our things.

Outside the hospital, my wife sat in a wheelchair holding our daughter as I frantically loaded the car. We were tense! Anxious! Not since the Saigon airlift had two people been so eager to just leave. Until we were in the car and moving, I kept expecting a group of hospital interns to burst through the doors and drag us back to Dr. Frankenstein's laboratory. As we pulled away from the hospital entrance, I breathed a sigh of relief. Happy to finally be leaving, I looked in the rearview mirror to catch a glimpse of Emerson sleeping in her car seat, my wife Meredith by her side. *At last,* I thought, *my family is going home.*

The Maternity Ward: Takes 2 & 3

My second child, William, was born in 2005. His younger brother, Carson, arrived a little less than two years later in 2007. Both of the boys had health issues that kept us concerned for a day or two in the hospital. William had a heart valve that wasn't opening and closing correctly. The infant heart specialist said it was a common condition for newborns and that it should clear itself up. Thank God, it did. As for Carson, he swallowed too much fluid during his mother's C-section and wasn't breathing right. He had to spend a night in the neonatal intensive care unit (NICU). Again, God blessed us and Carson was out of there in just over twenty-four hours.

The biggest thing I remember about Carson's brief stay in the NICU is Meredith's determination to see him. Because of his breathing, she didn't get a chance to look at him for more than a second after her surgery. While I split my time between visiting Carson downstairs and checking on Meredith's recovery on the maternity floor, Meredith was stuck in the room. With each hour that passed she grew more frustrated and angry about not being able to see her baby. Finally, at about 7:00 p.m., she'd had enough. Meredith crawled out of bed, grabbed her IV stand, and headed out the door. She didn't care that just twelve hours earlier she'd been cut open and unpacked like a gym bag. Mooning the world through the back of her fashionable hospital gown, my wife set off down the hall, resolved to see her son and prepared to inflict physical harm on anyone attempting to stop her.

When we stepped off the elevator and arrived at the NICU desk, I told the receptionist that we were there to see our son, Carson Howard. The young lady looked my wife up and down and asked, "Ma'am, should you be down here in your condition?" Then, in a voice eerily similar to Darth Vader's, my wife leaned as best she could over the desk, stared deeply into this poor, unfortunate creature's eyes, and stated in a manner that I am sure still terrifies that young woman to this day: *"LET ME SEE MY SON!"*

For a moment, the receptionist stared back in shocked silence (probably using the time to wet herself and watch her life flash before her eyes). Then, with no further objections, she buzzed us in. Although we made a couple of more visits to the NICU, the receptionist never again asked Meredith why she was there or whether or not she should be. Fearing the wrath of the dark side of the Force, she'd just look away, buzz the door open, and let Darth Vader pass.

With or Without the Bun

As infants, boys and girls aren't that different. They both cry. They're both tiny. And, when they're breastfed, they both poop enough yellow liquid to make you never want mustard on your hamburger again. Perhaps the biggest difference from a parent's perspective is the whole question of circumcision. Obviously, with girls, this is not an issue. But with boys you have to decide if you want your son's hotdog with or without the bun. We voted for without. After all, I'm circumcised (probably more information than you wanted to know), and we'd heard that there were some health advantages to having the procedure done. So, after consideration, Meredith and I decided go the circumcision route.

A change in hospital policies meant that I was not allowed to be present during Carson's circumcision. But I was present during William's. Although I had been advised by some that I should not witness William's circumcision because of how graphic it might be, I decided that I wanted to be there with my boy. Sure it might be hard to watch, but William is my firstborn son. I wanted to be by his side, offering support. And so, I went. I now know why God doesn't allow us to remember the things that happened to us when we were infants. If we did, every circumcised male would be in therapy. Talk about having issues to work through:

> "Well, Doc, I think my problem trusting people goes back to the day my parents let a mysterious, masked man slice off part of my penis with a razor blade."

Along with memories of breastfeeding, I don't know of anything that would be more difficult to get over than circumcision. Thank goodness that God mercifully inflicts amnesia on us when it comes to our infant years.

William's circumcision was brief but intense. As the physician grabbed his little foreskin with a pair of tweezers and pulled it forward, my son looked up at me as if to say, "Yo, Dad! Are you seeing this?" Then, with a quick snip, it was done. William let out a scream only dogs could hear. It broke my heart. I knew the doctor was doing what we wanted, but still, to watch my child screaming so hard that he couldn't even make a noise brought tears to my eyes. I felt like a heel. I felt like William had counted on me and, in his little mind, I'd let him down.

Within a few moments we were back in the hospital room. The tip of William's tiny penis was rose-red and slick with enough Vaseline to star in the Smurfs' production of *Grease*. As Meredith slept, I just sat there holding my son. Exhausted and no doubt still mad, he stared back at me in silence. I could just imagine what he would have said to me if he'd been able:

> "So, you're my dad, right? You're the guy who's responsible for looking after me—protecting me? Well, kinda dropped the ball on this one, didn't ya, Ace? Just so you'll know, if you ever again see someone approaching my private parts with a sharp blade of any kind, that definitely falls into the FOR GOD'S SAKE, DAD! DO SOMETHING! category. Are we clear?"

Sure thing, Son. No problem.

A Deer Caught in Headlights

In short, don't be surprised and try not to get too frustrated when your caveman acts like a deer caught in headlights on the maternity ward. It's an environment where he controls almost nothing. He doesn't always know what to do. Should he take a stand and insist that nurses not enter the room in the middle of the night? Should he defy the doctor and declare that he and his new mom are leaving because she feels fine despite the suggestion that she stay until her temperature is lower? Should he step out of the room while the lactation specialist squeezes mommy's breasts or continue to sit there, awkwardly pretending to watch television or read a magazine? It's all so unclear ... especially to someone who can't reheat the grits without burning himself.

Chapter 9:
Cavemen in Babyland

Before parenthood, I generally found excrement, mucus, and vomit disgusting. I did my best to avoid touching my own, much less another human being's. As a parent, you don't enjoy such a luxury. Human secretions become a way of life. If I could find a way to harness doo-doo, snot, or drool as an alternative fuel source, I'd make billions just off my kids.

When you're a mom or dad, you have to be willing to roll up your sleeves, grab some tissues, and touch things that once made your stomach turn. There's no way around it; you have no choice but to parent-up and deal with whatever needs cleaning, sanitizing, or absorbing. Being a parent means trading in your weak stomach for a box of wet wipes and a laundry basket full of booger-stained shirts.

This Ain't Our Daddies' Babyland

Nowadays, the parental duties like changing diapers, giving baths, rocking children to sleep, and getting up in the middle of the night to calm a screaming infant are usually shared by both parents. That's great. In my opinion, that's the way it should be. We dads should be more than happy to do our part. The thing to remember, however, is that many of us young fathers were raised by dads of a very different generation. My father was born in 1940, my mother in 1941. When my parents were young adults, their generation was still holding to the standard that dads earned the living while moms stayed home and handled the kids. Dads didn't give the baths, wipe crying eyes, or get up to deal with the occasional nightmare. That was mommy duty.

Don't get me wrong. My dad was an involved father—a real family man. He spent time with us, took us fishing, played ball in the backyard, took us to ballgames, and showed up for every school event we ever participated in. Both my parents were great. But Mom was the one who handled bath times, diaper changes, snotty noses, and post-puking clean-up projects. My mother was fine with that arrangement. Her reasoning was that Dad worked hard all day at the office, so she would handle things on the home front. Times have changed. Today's young dads are operating in a different world. This ain't our daddies' Babyland.

Today, being an involved father includes taking part in the day-to-day parenting tasks. Many women aren't stay-at-home mommies. They work outside the home too. They need and rightfully expect Daddy's help.

Even if you are a stay-at-home mom, the duties of parenthood are 24/7. Sure, there may be times when you want to help your husband get some rest or give him a break from the kids so he can decompress or prepare a presentation for work. But most days you're going to need him to help out and provide some back-up. That's okay. We guys should help. Just remember that, depending on how old your caveman is, he might be the first guy in his family to have children under this modern-day parenting paradigm. He might have no memory of a father who helped clean up after the kids or picked up around the house. He might even take some abuse from members of an older generation who view him as hen-pecked or see you as too demanding because he takes on many of the responsibilities that, forty years ago, were predominantly considered "Mommy's work." So be ready. It may take him some time to adapt to and get comfortable in his new role.

Diaper Wars

Poop and pee are, of course, two of the main bodily excretions that one becomes familiar with as a young parent. The rapid production of infant pee and poopage makes changing diapers a lot like playing paintball unarmed. You open a full diaper to find it saturated with gross, liquidy, disgusting residue. But that's no guarantee that the child is actually finished. Chances are, it's a trap—a cruel hoax designed to get you to remove the diaper so that your precious angel can then pummel you with even more baby waste the moment you're in range. The chamber of the gun isn't really empty; it's cocked and reloaded, fiendishly awaiting the moment fresh air hits your baby's bottom, alerting him or her that you are in the cross-hairs, and he or she is free to fire at will.

Undiapered babies aren't like trained marksmen aiming to take out a carefully selected target. No, they're more like green berets with orders to wipe out an entire enemy camp. "Poop on 'em all and let God sort 'em out!" A first-time dad is a sitting duck. It takes time to master the art of the quick diaper change. Sure, he did all right on that doll in parenting class. But that doll didn't flail, scream, and kick the petroleum jelly out of his hand every time he tried to gift-wrap its loins.

Changing a real baby is totally different. A young dad in the midst of a diaper change is like a lone soldier sprinting across open terrain, all the while knowing that enemy snipers are somewhere in the surrounding brush. He knows he has only a limited window of opportunity to get in, complete his mission, and get out without taking a hit. Frantically rushing against time, your caveman gets one side of a clean diaper fastened. Almost there; the safety of camp is in sight! Then, just yards away from home base, *rat-tat-tat-tat-tat.* He's hit! Dad down! Like a slow-motion scene from a Rambo movie, he can hear himself screaming "Noooooooo!" as he looks to see himself, the wall, the changing table, and the deceptively peaceful looking portrait of your infant that sits on the nearby shelf, all covered in freshly fired rounds of baby waste!

Frantically grabbing baby wipes as fast as he can, this wounded daddy warrior then scrambles in vain to clean himself as brownish goo runs down the sleeves of his former favorite shirt. After a valiant—albeit unsuccessful—effort, he finally manages to clean the child enough to get a new diaper on. But it's an empty accomplishment. He knows he's been defeated. The enemy took the hill. The Alamo fell to Santa Anna. In short, your caveman has just become another casualty of the diaper wars.

Daddying-Up for Bath Times

The changing table is not the only danger zone young dads are expected to venture into. Bath time can be another gruesome experience. Your child, after all, is an amphibious warrior, capable of firing on both land and sea.

When your caveman arrives home from work, he's tired. He's worked long hours. Chances are he's been yelled at by his boss, a client, or both at least once during the day. He wishes that you, his child's mother, would handle the baby's bath that night.

Of course, if he's truly honest with himself and has any sensitivity toward his wife at all, he knows that asking Mommy to handle bath time every night is not a fair expectation. If you're a stay-at-home mom, then you've already been with the baby all day. On the other hand, if you work a job, then you're just as tired when you get home as he is. If you're like most moms, you've breastfed until your nipples hurt. You've been burped on, peed on, pooped on, and vomited on more times than a fraternity house sofa. Perhaps you met your caveman at the door when he arrived home after work, holding the child out in front of you for him to take the moment he walked through the door. Before you became parents, you used to welcome him home with a warm smile and phrases like, "Hi, Honey, how was your day?" Now "Thank God!" tends to be the standard greeting. The look in your eyes tells him that you're exhausted and at your wits' end. He knows that even the suggestion that you bathe the kids because *he's* tired would no doubt result in a bloodbath not witnessed since Pol Pot's killing fields. So, he does the safest thing, rather than the easiest: he handles bath time.

A Little Poop, A Little Pee, A Little Lookin' the Other Way

As babies, kids aren't much company during bath time. You talk to them, but they just look up at you in terror, praying you don't let them drown. Baby bath times are all work and little conversation. Many nights, they go pretty smoothly. Babies aren't that big. They don't take that long to bathe.

But this brings me back to poop. Few things are as disheartening as having your baby doo-doo in the tub. After devoting time and energy to getting the water just right, you roll up your sleeves and wash your infant from head to foot. You're just about to pour the final cup of water over his or her tiny body to rinse off the soap when it happens. You suddenly notice that your baby is floating in a brownish-yellowy sludge. Unless you live in New Jersey, you know it's not the water. A curse word streaks across your mind (and, perhaps, your lips). All the while, your baby looks up at you with an "I've been waiting for just the right moment to do that" grin. Reluctantly, you do the only thing you can. You lift the child out of the water, wipe him or her off, drain the tub, and start over.

When the baby poops in the tub, there is no question what a daddy must do. The poop's right there. It's disgusting. You can't rationalize letting the baby sit in doo-doo filled water. You have to start again. Pee, however, is another issue. This raises an ethical question that all dads who help with bath times will inevitably face: what to do when the baby pees in the tub. One can never underestimate the effect of exhaustion in such baby-parent scenarios. It's the exhaustion that makes you do things—or, at least, consider doing things—that you normally never would.

The pee-pee dilemma arises after a father gets the baby in the tub and begins to wash him or her. At first, everything is fine. Then, Dad sees it. The water around the baby's private parts is rippling. Dad knows what's happening; the little booger is peeing in the tub. The bath is nearly done, but there's still rinsing to do, and your caveman now knows that there's urine in the water. For a second, he tries to convince himself that the rippling didn't happen. Next, he tries telling himself that it could have been caused by something else. But he knows. Damn his eyes! He knows.

Now comes the choice: does he drain the bath and start over, or does he convince himself that it's not that much pee and simply finish bathing the baby? Finishing the bath is much faster, much easier. It's also gross. Starting over is more sanitary, arguably more loving. The pee, however, is not visible. The kid doesn't know, nor does he or she care that there is pee-pee in the bath water. Mom might care, but she is not in the room and has no idea what is happening. She's downstairs, probably on the phone with a urologist and scheduling her husband's vasectomy so that "days like today" never happen again. Nope, only Daddy and his conscience are aware of the choice at hand. On one of his shoulders sits an angel whispering, "Start the bath over. You're the little fellow's daddy, for goodness sake. Surely you won't use this water knowing there's urine in it." On the other shoulder sits a devil. "Screw 'em," he snickers. "The kid's the one who peed in the tub!"

In my earliest days as a parent, I listened more to the angel. But, I have to confess, after five babies, two-hundred seventy-four thousand baths, and a seven-year, nonstop state of exhaustion, that devil's arguments have started making a lot more sense. I eventually developed what I call the *Senses Rule*. If I didn't hear it, don't see it, and can't smell it, then who cares about the ripples in the tub—it didn't happen. The kid will live. Bath time's not stopping. Sound gross? Maybe it is. But don't forget; gross is strictly a matter of perspective in Babyland.

Hey, Babies Are Worth It

I don't have time to go into all the grossities that accompany being a parent. It's safe to say they multiply as your baby grows into toddlerhood. All I can say is, unless you are rich enough to hire a live-in maid or you're married to an obsessive-compulsive person who doesn't sleep, cleanliness is going to take a beating when you have kids. Your once-clean vehicle becomes a food bank on wheels. Milk stains and regurgitated formula decorate your car seats and furniture. You buy Lysol and disinfectant by the barrel. Laundry multiplies like a virus, engulfing your home in a pandemic of dirty baby clothes, spit-up-on shirts, and fluid-stained trousers.

Is having a baby worth all the changes and modifications? You bet! It's not even close. After all, where's the adventure in a day that doesn't involve hurrying to change a diaper before baby feces is launched across a room at bazooka-like speed? Whenever the mess seems unbearable and I feel like I'm starting to lose my patience, I try to remember how blessed I am. There are a lot of people living in clean houses and driving spotless cars who would love to change places with me. They'd gladly put up with several months of late-night lullabies or trade their Lexus for a minivan if it meant they could experience the love and memories that accompany even one day in Babyland.

The "Daddy Way"

The one heads-up I want to give new mommies in this chapter is actually a piece of advice that I would recommend you carry with you throughout your parental life. It will only become truer as you enter the toddler and young-child stages. If you are going to expect your caveman to help carry the load (and well you should), then be prepared to let him do it the "daddy way." Few things irritate a father more than being told that he needs to do more to help with the kids, only to be lectured about how he's "not doing it right" whenever he tries to give a bath, dress the baby, or serve the applesauce. Is your method better? Probably so. After all, you're Mom. Most likely, you're the chief baby caretaker and expert childcare provider in your home. But that doesn't mean your caveman's way won't work. As long as his approach gets the job done, I'd recommend you look away and let him go with it.

Look, if you want your caveman to be involved in kid maintenance, I'm all for it. But you gotta be willing to give up some control. It's not essential that he do everything exactly the way you would. Don't expect a caveman to be enthusiastic about doing his part if he knows that his method is inevitably going to be criticized. Sure, if he's about to suffocate your son by putting a diaper on his head or is moments away from poisoning your daughter by feeding her fanny-rash cream, then feel free to step in and say something. But if it's just that he doesn't give a bath the way you do, grabs a different pair of jammies than you would have, or elects to sing "Twinkle, Twinkle Little Star" instead of "Itsy Bitsy Spider" as a lullaby, then consider biting your lip and letting him try it his way. Otherwise, what you mistake for a lack of desire to help with the baby may actually just be the impending dread of having you point out what he "should have done differently" every time he tries to make a parental move in Babyland.

Chapter 10:
Sleepless in Babyland

My wife and I are tired. In fact, we've been tired for more than eight years. I can't remember what life was like when we weren't tired. When you have babies or small children, you live your life in a haze of exhaustion. Have babies and small children at the same time, and sleep becomes almost as rare as a conservative political opinion out of Hollywood. There's always a diaper to change, a nose to wipe, a spill to clean up, or a catastrophe to attend to. You get the older kids naked for bath time. Then, as soon as you turn your back to tend to the baby, they disappear out the bathroom door. You stop what you're doing and chase them into the bedroom, only to be greeted by the sight of tiny butts and private parts flopping about in a pile of your previously clean laundry. There are meal times, story times, prayer times … all good stuff, but stuff that takes energy. No doubt about it, one of your biggest adjustments as young parents will be learning to live with sleep deprivation.

Sleep Is for the Weak (and Fortunate)

The truth is that the first few years of parenthood are a lot like being interrogated as a prisoner of war: you have limited freedom; you're rarely allowed to sleep; and you're constantly being yelled at in languages you can't understand. The only difference is that prisoners of war can give up information that will bring an end to the cruelty. With an infant or toddler, there's nothing you can do. Most of the time, I'm more than ready to tell my children anything they want to know. But the horrible reality is that they don't want to know anything. They just want more of my time and energy. They're not even aware that they've defeated me in psychological warfare. They just keep wanting, needing, demanding.

Nope, parents can't reason, bargain, or confess their way to a good night's sleep. The only way through the parental gauntlet is to put your head down, tighten your chinstrap, repeat over and over, "Sleep is for the weak," and barrel ahead. Straight through! Endure! Persevere! That's being a sleep-deprived mom or dad. The way you know there's a God is that He miraculously makes the blessings of parenthood so awesome that, in the end, you wouldn't give it up for anything in the world.

Different DNA?

For all the pride we men take in being the physically stronger sex, we're the ones who usually crack first when consistently denied sleep. One or two nights of very little sleep, and I'm barely able to say my own name. My wife, on the other hand, is superhuman. As a new mom, she could stay up almost all night for five or six nights in a row and still not miss a beat. When William was a baby, I'll bet the woman didn't sleep more than three hours a night for a year. I did my share of night duty too, but nothing like her. And I complained five times as much.

Maybe women just have something in their DNA that allows them to function without sleep once they have a baby. If so, we cavemen sure wish some scientist would hurry up and find it so we could use that bit of medical knowledge to our advantage. You'd better believe we'd play that card. How awesome would it be for men if we could say with a clear conscience that we would gladly get up and feed the baby at night, if only we were genetically made for it?

Of course, women don't want such a gene discovered—even if it exists. You women want men to know that you can endure more than us, but you want us to think it's because you're tougher. That's because, if it's just about toughness, you can still shame us into action. Cavemen aren't stupid. We know what you're doing. We realize that when you nudge us at three-thirty in the morning and say, "Honey, I've been up all night with the baby, can you get him this time?" what you're really saying is:

> "Come on, tough guy! I've been up half the night nursing and nurturing YOUR screaming child; now

it's your turn. Put on your panties, get out of bed, and tend to the baby, you sleep-hoarding wuss! What's the matter, you big sissy? Can't handle it? Are you gonna cry?"

As men, even if we are going to cry (and don't think I haven't wanted to), we have to get up. It's a matter of honor. We know it's not fair to make mommies do all the work. We realize we can't expect the women to handle all the late night duties— *UNLESS THERE'S A BIOLOGICAL DIFFERENCE.* Oh, if only modern medicine would give us guys something we could work with.

The Lie-Off

Of course, while you mommies might be tougher prisoners of war than us, you're still prisoners of war. Funny thing about prisoners: they often turn on one another. Having a baby or small children is like being under siege. Little people have you surrounded. Your supply lines are cut. Naps, clean cars, adult conversations, and tidy houses aren't allowed in. You have to live off what you've got. That means there's a limited sleep supply. Mom and Dad have to fight it out. Thus begins a whole series of rituals and contests as both sides vie for sleep, time, and a chance to take a break.

The Lie-Off is a test of wills that commonly takes place between new mommies and daddies. It mostly occurs during the first year of parenthood. Here's how the lie-off works:

It's the dead of night. You're both asleep (finally). Suddenly, you hear it—the baby is crying. You lie there, as still as death, your face turned away from your significant other. Your eyes are open, but as far as your spouse knows, you're still asleep. If you're a veteran of the lie-off, you may even make fake snoring noises. But this is a tricky maneuver, best only attempted by real professionals. If your snores don't sound authentic, you'll be busted and find yourself singing Barney the Dinosaur's "I Love You, You Love Me" song to a screaming infant at two in the morning. Most of the time, I just use the silent method.

Regardless, you continue to lie motionless, your ears tuned in to both your child and any sound of movement from the other side of your bed. Meanwhile, the baby's cries grow louder, piercing the dark night more and more with every passing moment. You know your spouse must hear it, but you can't say anything because that will give away the fact that you hear it too. You both remain quiet, each calling the other's bluff, each trying to convince the other that you are too deep in sleep to hear the child. All the while, you both know that the other is doing exactly the same thing. It's a parent's game of chicken. Who'll blink first? Who'll roll out of bed and tend to the baby before the neighbors hear the screaming and call social services?

Oh, how far you've fallen. There you lie, two grown adults who stood before a preacher and a congregation of family and friends, vowing to love each other to the end of time. You promised to lay down your lives for each other—till death do you part. Perhaps you even wrote your own vows in which you talked of how you would cross the hottest desert, swim the widest ocean, and climb to the snow-covered peaks of the highest mountains just to serve and adore your long searched-for soul mate. Now you're lying in bed faking sleep, ready to sell out the love of your life for those few extra minutes of slumber that are so precious in Babyland.

Sometimes, I win the lie-off. Sometimes, Meredith does. The point is, when a city is surrounded by a foreign army and can't get food, you don't share your sandwich as quickly as you used to. When you have an infant or small kids, stealing a few moments of sleep is like clinging protectively to that last bite of grilled cheese.

A Babyland Divided Cannot Stand

Sleep deprivation often gives birth to arguments that you and your caveman never could have imagined having before kids. Meredith and I argued before we were parents, of course; but those arguments tended to be bona fide, adult disagreements. We argued about money, whose turn it was to take out the trash, or what movie to go see. But again, as you have children, your patience and brain cells decrease proportionally. Meredith and I have gone rounds over what jammies the baby should wear, whether or not to use the Elmo or the Blue's Clues towels, whose fault it is for forgetting to stock the baby's changing table with Butt Paste, and what the number of the day was that morning on *Sesame Street*.

One time, Meredith got so mad at me that she actually un-invited me to my own daughter's birthday party. I don't remember all the details, but I do remember that it was late, I was tired, and so was Meredith. The confrontation happened after we had just gotten our kids to bed. It had been a long, exhausting day. All I wanted to do was flop in front of the television and think about nothing except what I was watching. Meredith, on the other hand, had other plans. What I had looked forward to as downtime, Meredith envisioned as a chance to share with me all she had planned for Emerson's party. I don't recall exactly what started the fight. No doubt I was probably the main one at fault. I'm sure I was being my selfish, barely attentive self. Meredith probably wanted me to listen as she described the party hats she'd picked out or asked my opinion about when to serve the cake. All I remember is that the argument escalated fast. Before I knew it, I was storming into the kitchen yelling, "I just want to watch ten minutes of Sportscenter!"

"Oh, that's really helpful!" Meredith sarcastically responded. "I think I'll run right out and nominate you for

Husband of the Year!" Meredith knew that comment would punch my buttons, and she punched them with both fists.

Then, in anger, I yelled something I shouldn't have. The moment I said it, I knew I'd made a dumb decision. I felt myself reaching to grab my words the moment they escaped my lips—but it was too late! The next thing I knew, a huge bowl of popcorn was flying through the air straight at my head.

"You are not to come to my daughter's birthday party!" Meredith screamed. "Do you hear me, you jerk!"

"The heck I won't!" I shot back. "She's my daughter. I'll be at her birthday party—front and center!"

"You'd better not!" Meredith retorted.

"How are you going to stop me? This is my house!"

"I'll call the police if I have to! I'll get a restraining order! You will *NOT* be at that party!"

Now it was on! "Not only will I be at the party," I defiantly replied, "I'll be the one holding the cake when she blows out the candles!"

"You'll not touch that cake!"

"Oh yes I will! I'll be holding the cake, wearing a big flippin' party hat, and singing 'Happy Cotton-Pickin' Birthday' at the top of my lungs!"

Red with rage, Meredith pointed a stern finger right in my face. "I'll make sure you don't come to Emerson's party! I'll change the locks on the house while you're at work if I have to!"

"Go ahead," I smugly answered, "it's a *COOKOUT!*"

Thus, the conversation spiraled downward: two normally mature adults—yelling, throwing bowls of popcorn, threatening restraining orders, and holding a toddler's birthday party hostage. I'm not saying that sleep deprivation excuses our behavior; I'm just saying it was a factor.

Of course, both Meredith and I have long since apologized to one another for our behavior that night. I'm also happy to report that Meredith reconsidered and allowed me to come to the party without forcing me to defy a court order. She even let me hold the cake after all. The point is this: be on your guard. You and your caveman can't let sleep deprivation become a dividing force in your relationship. You've got to stick together if you hope to survive. A Babyland divided cannot stand.

The Sleep-Deprived Caveman

It's important to remember that sleep-deprived cavemen often say dumb things they don't really mean. For men, the first thing that usually goes is our patience. But right behind it and running a close second is our good sense. Given that women often perceive us to be insensitive boneheads when we're well rested, you can imagine (or perhaps already know from firsthand experience) how jerk-like we cavemen appear to the average female once sleep goes out the window.

Sleep-deprived cavemen tend to be complainers. We make sure people know how tired we are, how difficult a time we've had getting up in the middle of the night to soothe a crying baby, or how challenging it is to take on parental tasks after we've been working all day. We might suffer less sleep deprivation than mommies, but we can also handle less (or, at least, we act like we can). Sleep-deprived daddies are notorious for snapping at our wives, snapping at our friends, rolling our eyes at reasonable requests, ignoring the smell of baby poop for extended periods in hopes that Mommy will "notice it first," cursing diapers that won't fasten, threatening baby bottles that leak, and babbling like morons whenever we can't find the remote to the television (which, nine times out of ten, we're sitting on). Such behavior doesn't necessarily mean that we're totally insane. No, we're just mentally and physically drained. And, as you women well know, a mentally and physically drained caveman is not a pretty sight.

The good thing is that, as dads, we do learn to adapt. We learn to sleep when we can. We take power naps during our lunch hour. We lean the seat back in our car and snooze for ten minutes before leaving the parking lot at work. Most fathers are surprised to learn how well they can sleep in chairs, at their desks, leaning against walls, in nursery gliders, or hiding in their driveways before entering the house to take on their end-of-the-workday daddy duties. Eventually, we accept that sleep deprivation is part of life in Babyland. It's the cost of being a dad. And, truth be told, it's worth it.

Chapter 11:
Cavemen at Work

This chapter discusses the challenges associated with returning to work after a baby is born. Specifically, this chapter focuses on the tensions that can arise when new daddies go back to work. It's true that, these days, many new mommies return to work after only a few weeks of maternity leave. Such moms usually rely on daycare or a trusted friend or family member to help with the baby. But in many families, one of the parents (usually the mom) elects to stay home or significantly reduce his or her work hours in order to serve as the new baby's primary caregiver. This chapter predominantly addresses the friction that arises between moms who function as the primary caregivers and dads who are trying to adjust to working in a post-baby world.

So What Do You Do?

It's no secret that most men take their jobs seriously. Of course, we live in a day and age when many women are devoted to their careers as well. Women are CEOs of large corporations, successful entrepreneurs, and accomplished professionals. As more and more females are deservedly climbing the corporate ladder and crashing through glass ceilings, our American society is finally learning to applaud and recognize women who are successful in their professions.

Yet, while many women are very successful in their careers, most people usually don't define a woman first and foremost by her professional status. Even among the professionally accomplished women I know, most females don't attach their self-esteem to their jobs the way males do. For men, things are a bit different. We still live in a culture in which society as a whole tends to judge and define men by what they do for a living, how successful they are at their jobs, and how much money they make. If women meet each other for the first time at a social event, their initial conversations often center on family, where they got their outfits, how they each know their host, and so on. When two men meet at the same event, you can bet the conversation won't progress more than two minutes before one guy asks the other, "So, what do you do?"

Right or wrong, men's self-esteem often rises or falls with how important they feel their jobs are and how successful they perceive themselves to be. The pressure guys experience to feel like they are succeeding on the job only increases once they have a baby. That's because men like to feel that they are being good providers for their families. Even if a guy is married to a wife who brings home more money than him or owns her own business, he wants to believe that he is doing his part to be responsible and take care of his wife and kids. In other words, men want to feel proud of what they do.

Of course, we also live in a time when more and more men are becoming stay-at-home dads—especially if their wives have thriving careers. There's nothing wrong with that. Truth be told, one of my dreams is to become successful enough as a writer that I can be a stay-at-home dad who writes while my kids are in school. That way, I can be around to care for my children while my wife is free to pursue any career she wants. But even in that scenario, I still want to write. I still want a career. I've still got to feel like a breadwinner. I think most guys would tell you that they feel the same way.

I mention all this because a caveman's return to work after a baby arrives can be a tricky maneuver which can cause tension and conflict between new moms and dads. Avoiding and reconciling disagreements requires open communication. Many of the problems Meredith and I have encountered in this area have boiled down to one very simple thing: we've often been the victims of our own differing expectations.

Caveman Esteem

I can't overstate the point I made earlier: men tend to buy into the idea that "we are what we do." During my eight-plus years as a dad, I've worked as a minister, a salesman, a teacher, a staff writer, a marriage and parenting coach, a freelance writer, and a published author. In between, I've experienced down times and periods when I was unemployed. I've known times when I scraped to find any gig I could that would pay enough to put food on the table.

One of the hardest points in my life came about a year after my daughter, Emerson, was born. After resigning from the ministry for reasons I thought best for my family, I took a cold-call sales position. I now know what people in hell do for a living. Many folks are very good at sales and—for reasons that are beyond me—even enjoy it. God bless 'em. I just couldn't do it. For one, I was working on 100 percent commission. While commission sales offer the prospect of a big payday down the line, it's a tough way to pay the bills when you're just starting out and don't have much money in the bank. Inevitably, "selling to survive" just became too burdensome. Add the fact that I wasn't a natural salesman, and my life soon spiraled into a series of miserable days.

Finally, after a year in sales, I threw in the towel. I ended up exhausting much of my savings and taking a job working in a friend's coffee shop to make ends meet. All the while, I slid further and further into depression. There I was, in my mid-thirties and convinced that I was already washed up. Sure I had an awesome wife who stuck by me and a beautiful baby girl, but in my selfish state of mind I could only see my failures. My life just didn't seem to matter.

That's when a well-meaning friend named Jack started trying to "encourage" me. Jack had a great job with a major company, an incredible family, and, to this day, doesn't possess a selfish bone in his body. He's a strong Christian, an awesome dad, and a great example of a husband. I have no doubt that he had only the best intentions each time he talked to me and tried to lift my spirits. Jack constantly shared with me the story of how he, as a young husband and father, once had to clean pools just to pay the bills. He told me how hopeless he'd sometimes felt and how hard times had been. But through faith in God, hard work, and a refusal to quit, he eventually saw the light at the end of the tunnel and made a better life for himself and his family.

Much of what Jack had to say about faith and perseverance was absolutely true. In addition, I know that he was only trying to help each time he shared his past struggles with me. But it got to the point where, if I heard that pool-scrubbing story one more time, I was going to run out and apply for a job cleaning pools too—just so I could drown myself! Anger and resentment built up inside me. Everything in me just wanted to scream:

"Enough with the doggone pool story! You now have a good job! You have a future! Yeah, it's great that you made it, but I haven't. What if I don't? While you sit there in your nice white-collar world behind a comfortable desk all day, I'm busy fielding complaints from soccer moms who don't think there's enough froth on their cappuccinos! You have a real career. You bring home a decent paycheck every month. Meanwhile, I'm stuck making eight bucks an hour and pouring drinks I can't even pronounce! You've got colleagues who own stock and take their families on vacations. I'm working with a high school drop-out who insists I call him 'Venom' and won't stop trying to explain to me how the X-men could really happen. Please, just shut up!"

All the while, my wife Meredith couldn't understand why I was turning into the grumpiest dork on the face of the earth. She felt the financial pinch too, but she could see how temporary it was and continually expressed her certainty that I would eventually find my career and be successful. She just appreciated that I was doing what I could until something better came along.

While Meredith's attitude was no doubt better than mine, it also shed light on a common disconnect between moms and dads. Most moms can separate their worth as a parent from what they do for a career. For dads, however, the two tend to be inseparably intertwined. To cavemen, the ability to bring home a decent paycheck, provide for their families' financial needs, and hold a job they can feel proud of is directly tied to their roles and responsibilities as fathers. For most men, slumping in a career or losing a job translates into feelings of failure as a husband and dad.

This is a key difference that can often create frustration and lead to conflict. Mom often wants Dad to work less once the baby arrives. She wants him home and focused on the family. She needs her caveman's help and desires for him to spend time with their child. Dad, on the other hand, often feels the pressure to work more. Why? Now there's another mouth to feed, another body to clothe, and another human being's future to plan and provide for. It's not that Dad doesn't want to cut his work days short so he can be with the family; it's just that he now feels more than ever that he needs to increase his income, earn a promotion, or make his business more profitable. To Mom, Daddy seems too consumed with his job (and maybe he is). To Dad, all the work seems like a necessary part of being a responsible parent.

Baby's Here, Now Back to Work

One mistake that a new father may make is thinking that, once the baby is home and Dad has taken a few days off to help Mom adjust, he can then simply jump right back into his normal work routine without it causing any problems. To some extent, the return to "work as usual" might be necessary, such as when your caveman answers to a boss who expects him back at his desk and performing as before once the standard paternity leave is over. Of course, even in those cases, Dad is in for a rude awakening. It's a lot different trying to make a presentation at work or be sharp for a business meeting once you have a baby who's kept you up all night. Long days at the office and business trips out of town are no longer merely unfortunate separations from a spouse. Now they're scenarios that produce more work for Mommy and, potentially, feelings of resentment toward Daddy. Things Mommy once accepted with only minor protests now sometimes become major points of contention in the relationship.

The tensions tend to become more magnified if Mommy is returning to work too. Prior to baby, your caveman was probably thrilled that you were pursuing your career, particularly if you brought home a good income and your job didn't interfere with his work schedule. Now that there's a little one in the picture, Mommy's decision to go back to work requires more give and take from Daddy. This can cause stress for a man who defines his worth as a husband and father by how successful he is in his job. Without question, working moms have a right to expect their husbands to bend some in order to allow *both* spouses to get back to work. Just know that the transition can be tough for many dads because they underestimate the impact fatherhood will have on their pace of corporate ladder-climbing.

Hopefully, understanding how men view themselves and their role as fathers will encourage women to appreciate *why* men are eager to get back to work. This doesn't mean that women are wrong for thinking their new dads should work less or be around more to help with the baby. It just means that knowing where dads are coming from might help mommies realize that they are probably not dealing with intentionally disengaged fathers. Odds are, your husband doesn't mean to communicate that he cares more about his career than he does his own family. Most likely, the reason he's working harder is for exactly the opposite reason; he thinks he's loving his family by trying to provide all he can for them.

Of course, dads who think this way are often sorely mistaken. I've known many a husband and father who has let work and climbing the corporate ladder become all-consuming. Sadly, such a man often wakes up one day to realize that he's sacrificed a relationship with his wife and kids to the gods of materialism and financial success. So please don't misunderstand me, my point is not to justify men's focus on their careers. Rather, I simply want to help moms understand the way we men think so that any concerns you have can be addressed as constructively as possible.

If you need to have an "I think you're working too much" discussion with your caveman, I would advise you to approach it cooperatively rather than combatively. Instead of viewing yourself as the lone concerned parent who needs to enlighten a selfishly career-focused hubby, try to view the discussion as being between two concerned parents who simply have different expectations regarding what it means to provide a loving, secure home for your child. My recommendation is that you focus on your caveman's loving intentions instead of on his outward actions. This replaces a negative, frustrated tone with a positive, trusting one. And, as we all know, couples who broach touchy subjects trusting and believing the best of each other tend to respond to each others' concerns better than those who enter a discussion angry, irritated, or using a tone that screams, "Change, you selfish numbskull!"

All a man usually needs in order to respond well to your concerns is this: communicate that you truly appreciate all his hard work and that you realize he's doing it for the family. If he feels such appreciation, chances are he'll listen to what you have to say and note what you'd like to see changed. It's when he feels his efforts aren't appreciated and he's being accused of a lack of caring that his defenses go up and he defaults into fight mode.

The Work-at-Home Caveman

If only your caveman worked from home. Then you and your spouse wouldn't experience all those work-related conflicts you and your new-mommy amigas discuss every Thursday morning at Starbucks. Right? *Wrong!* If a guy is self-employed or works from home, like I do, then it really gets challenging. The boundaries between work and home become blurred and open to interpretation. Such lack of clarity can fuel the fires of frustration.

Meredith sometimes can't understand why I have to work when I could take "just a minute or two" to tend to some issue regarding the kids. My response is to get angry and feel like Meredith has no understanding of what it takes for me to get my work done so that I can get paid and earn an income. My wife's mad because I seem content to leave all the daytime parenting to her. I'm boiling and mumbling under my breath because I feel she has no realistic comprehension of what it takes to build a business and support a family.

It's not that I don't want to be available to deal with all the situations or help with family demands that arise during the day. It's just that, last time I checked, my kids don't pay me very well. In fact, they're takers. My daughter has been living rent-free under my roof for eight years now. Except for a two-year phase in which she wanted to be a Disney princess, she hasn't even offered to get a job and help with the family expenses.

Meanwhile, William and Carson seem content to simply play and watch *Clifford the Big Red Dog* on public television. They've both expressed an interest in growing up to be Iron Man, but other than that, they have no ambition. No vision. No asking themselves, "What am I doing with my life?" Nope, they just want to have fun and bother their sister. Other than breaking the world's record for the most questions a five-year-old can ask his father in a two-hour period, William has no real goals. As for Carson, he just wants to destroy things, hide half-eaten pieces of candy in clean laundry, and insist that he doesn't have to pee even as he grabs his crotch and does his best rendition of *River Dance* in the middle of the grocery store.

And then there are the babies, Samuel and Asher. Every time I ask when they intend to find employment, they just slobber and regurgitate Cheerios.

My wife works as much as she can, but she and I agree that we want her devoting most of her attention to being a mom (a role at which she's very gifted). That means that earning the family income falls predominantly to me. I don't want to put work before my family, but reality dictates that I stay on task to keep the family budget above water.

I'm willing to bet that the Howards are like many other families in which Dad works from home. Mommy has difficulty understanding why her caveman can't happily take "just five minutes" to get the baby, change the baby, check on the baby, or help her carry in the things she just bought at the store for the baby. Daddy, meanwhile, grows more and more frustrated because he feels like Mommy is prepared to just-five-minute his entire day away as she continually breaks his train of thought and interrupts him as he tries to work.

Figuring It Out

If you're like a lot of couples, one of the first trials you will have to weather as new parents is the transition that occurs when

Daddy goes back to work. You, as the mom, will likely wonder why your caveman doesn't recognize that life is now very different, and everything—including his approach to work—will have to change. He, as the dad, can't understand how you expect him to buy diapers, pay the pediatrician co-pays, and save for college when you keep interrupting his work or get mad at him every time he needs to stay late at the office.

Solutions? Hey, I wish I could give you a standard formula that works. But the truth is, every mom and dad will have to figure this one out on their own. Like most things in life, it's probably going to take a lot of give and take. Your caveman needs to understand that there will be times when he'll need to take a stand to keep his priorities straight. He needs to make sure that work does not become more important than his family. If he works from home, then he must accept that family matters will occasionally demand his attention, even during the workday. Hopefully, with time and prayer, he'll learn wisdom, knowing when it's time to step out of the office to help Mommy and when it's time to lock the door and pretend he can't hear Armageddon occurring in the next room. Likewise, if he commutes to an office, he needs to realize that when he gets home his wife is going to need some backup. He can't simply walk through the door, kiss the wife and baby hello, and then flop into a recliner to relax after a long day. If he's in the habit of bringing work home with him, he's going to have to see that even the next day's reports often will have to wait until he's helped with baby.

As for you wives, I would suggest that you be aware of the challenge your caveman is facing. He's desperately trying to find the balance between earning a living and being there for his family. One thing that will help is to sit down together and discuss what "providing for our family" means. You may feel that $45,000 a year in income, a small house in need of some work, and a decent used car qualify as "providing," as long as your husband doesn't have to work more than forty hours a week and is home by six every night. Your caveman, on the other hand, might think that "providing" means making closer to $100,000 a year, buying a new car, purchasing a bigger house, and being in a position to send your kid to a private school—even if it means working sixty hours a week and constantly going on business trips. You and your caveman need to get on the same page. Reaching some agreement regarding your expectations is one important step to resolving any work-versus-family-related conflicts.

Also, get advice. You probably know other married couples whose marriages you respect and admire. Perhaps they're neighbors, members of your church, or long-time friends. Maybe you know a minister, professional counselor, or marriage coach you can consult. Talk to them. Be open about some of the struggles you're having in this and any other area of your marriage. You may be surprised and encouraged to learn how other couples struggle with the same things. Ask others how they handle the work-versus-family dilemma. I find that the first step to fixing many problems is simply gaining the peace of mind that my problems aren't as big or unusual as I originally thought. Heck, that's one of the biggest reasons I'm writing this book. I'm trying to assure expecting and new mommies that the frustrations and confusion they sometimes feel regarding their new daddies isn't unusual, and to empower them with some knowledge they can use to their advantage to keep their marriages happy and strong.

Finally, never forget the importance of talking to your caveman—OFTEN! Thanks to many open talks, I've come to understand that I need to be as flexible as I can with my schedule in order to be there for Meredith and the kids. Conversely, Meredith has grown to understand that she needs to help guard my work time by acting as a buffer between me and the children during certain times of the workday.

All of this, of course, is often easier said than done. Meredith and I have drawn boundaries, only to cross them and have to talk and redraw them again. My two cents' worth? No matter how hard and frustrating it gets, keep sharing feelings and expectations. Don't be shy about telling your caveman what you see and what you think. Oh, and when your caveman talks, be a good listener. He's got some valid feelings too.

Most likely, there will be arguments. But, hopefully, there will be plenty of apologies too. The key is to make sure that you don't let the sometimes conflicting demands of work and parenthood spark unresolved arguments that damage your marriage and family.

Chapter 12:
Caveman in the Middle

This chapter is devoted to briefly addressing one of the most delicate relationships known to humankind: the one between a new mommy and her mother-in-law. More specifically, it's meant to help a new mom understand a bit more about what her caveman is experiencing when tensions arise between the mother of his child and the woman who raised him.

Some women, of course, get along great with their mothers-in-law. For others, it's a swim upstream. I'm fortunate that my wife and my mother love each other and want to be around one another, at least most of the time. Meredith often goes out of her way to do little things for my mom, such as emailing pictures of the kids or looking for a gift she knows my mother will really appreciate. Recently, it was even Meredith's idea to invite my folks to join us on our family vacation. Conversely, Mom does things for Meredith too. She'll call when she knows of sales Meredith might want to be aware of or when she's read some article Meredith might find interesting. On more than one occasion, Mom has even made a point to compliment Meredith on her parenting skills.

Still, there are certain laws that govern the universe. Remove them, and chaos reigns. Gravity keeps the Earth and planets in orbit. No two objects can occupy the same space at the same time. $E=MC^2$. And, the arrival of grandkids creates tension between wives and mothers-in-law.

The fact is, once a woman has a baby, she becomes the latest initiate into a club to which her mother-in-law has belonged for decades. For some unfortunate reason, this reality often leads to tension and conflict between the two. Why? Best I can figure, it basically boils down to a case of motherly instincts meets generational differences. A young mom will inevitably have her own way of doing things. She has a certain structure and routine she abides by. She has set rules and guidelines for caring for her child. Simultaneously, her mother-in-law has already raised at least one kid and can easily interpret any rule or guideline that's different from the way she parented as a poorly veiled indictment of her own mothering abilities. When this happens, hurt feelings and irritated moods can abound. Even a new mommy and her mother-in-law who previously got along fine can suddenly find each other's comments about as appreciated as bluegrass fiddlers at the NAACP Image Awards. Unfortunately for cavemen, we often find ourselves caught in the middle.

Between Mother-in-Law Rock and New-Mommy Hard Place

Most confrontations between Meredith and my mother revolve around what constitutes proper expectations regarding the children. Since my daughter's birth, Meredith has been a zealot when it comes to taking care of our kids. She's up to speed on the latest medical research and recommendations. She knows what the kids should eat, what kinds of toys are the safest, and what programs the children should and should not watch on television. Meredith has declared war on sugar and soft drinks. God help any partially hydrogenated food dish that's foolish enough to try to sneak past her into our children's diets. I'm glad Meredith is a health-conscious mom. In a nation where more and more kids resemble video-game-playing versions of Jabba the Hut, I'm grateful for a wife who's mindful of making sure my kids eat right and don't spend too much time in front of the tube.

How can such convictions occasionally lead to conflict between Meredith and my mother? Well, Mom is old school. While she always made sure to feed us healthy dishes too, Mom comes from a generation when, if it once swam, flew, or walked on all fours, then it's fair game—just fry it and eat it! It's the same generation that used to drink and smoke while pregnant (my mother didn't), rode in cars with their babies on their laps instead of in car seats (my mother did), and actually believed the commercials that said Cocoa Puffs were part of a nutritious breakfast. My mother, God bless her, still thinks bacon is a food group. Don't get me wrong, I love it! I always like going to Mom's and getting a dose of the good ole fried stuff I ate growing up. Not that I don't like my wife's cooking too, but it's nice to occasionally eat a burger that was never part of the plant kingdom and drink milk I can't see through.

Unfortunately, my wife's and my mother's differing dietary expectations can make for some confrontational moments when it comes to the kids. Meredith sometimes feels frustrated because she wants Mom to be more selective of what she feeds the children. Mom sometimes feels insulted because, in her mind, Meredith's objections to her menu imply that she—a woman who raised three kids of her own—doesn't know how to properly care for children. And Kindred, who inevitably ends up caught between mother-in-law rock and new-mommy hard place, considers taking up chain smoking to deal with the stress.

But the conflicts arose long before our kids entered the eating-solid-food stage. They began soon after we brought Emerson home from the hospital. From the time the new baby first arrived, Meredith's and my mother's conflicting methods of parenting created friction. Emerson is my parents' oldest grandchild. When she was a baby, she was the only grandkid they had. Mom and Dad always wanted to hold the baby, show off the baby, let their friends hold the baby, and so on. Meredith, on the other hand, was very protective of Emerson. To be sure, she wanted Mom and Dad to hold their new granddaughter and enjoy being grandparents, but she didn't want the baby passed around like a hot potato or have tons of strange onlookers sticking their noses in Emerson's face and interfering with her routine.

Meredith had a strict regimen for Emerson. Nap times, bath times, feeding times, and bed times all happened according to a set schedule. Mom sometimes thought Meredith could be more flexible. She couldn't understand why the baby needed a bath *every day* or why Emerson couldn't stay awake a little longer, given that MaMa and PaPa had just arrived. New grandparents long to spoil and show off grandbabies. New mommies strive to establish some structure for their infants and protect them from overstimulation. Grandmothers want new mommies to mother the way they did. New mommies have their own ideas that often contradict what a mother-in-law pictured or thinks makes sense. It's kind of like the Fourth of July on an emotional level: there are plenty of fireworks to ignite, and all it takes is one small spark to set them off.

Poor Raymond

Another point of frustration for Meredith has been my relationship with my mother. Meredith accuses me of being a "momma's boy." My father and older brother agree with her. My dad thinks that mom pampers me more than him, and my brother has labeled me "Mom's favorite." The three of them have given me the nickname "Raymond"—as in *Everybody Loves Raymond*, the hit comedy I mentioned in chapter 1 about a man torn between marriage and his over-protective mother.

Perhaps I am a bit of a momma's boy. But what can I say, I'm close to my mother. Aren't most guys? After all, if it weren't for Mom's wisdom and warnings, who knows how many of us would have run with scissors to our death, lived our lives disfigured with pupils that froze cross-eyed, or endured the emotional trauma of being pulled from the burning wreckage of a near-death accident only to have it discovered that we *weren't* wearing clean underwear. It was Mom who'd lie down in our beds at night to make us feel safe after a nightmare. It was Mom who picked us up and comforted us after we fell and skinned our knees. And it was Mom who intervened to make sure Dad didn't kill us after he arrived home from work to discover the car covered in finger paint or find the garage on fire. Who can count the number of times Mom did her best to make a hamburger "just like the one at McDonald's," only to be met with the thankless tears of a crying child screaming, "That doesn't look like a Big Mac!" Am I a "Raymond?" Yes, I am! I do have a deep sense of loyalty and attachment to my mother. But what can I tell you— she earned it.

That being said, I firmly believe that my wife comes first. Meredith has never accused me of valuing Mom's opinion more than hers or caring more about my mother than I do my own spouse. It's mostly the way Mom treats me that causes Meredith to struggle. Whenever we visit my folks or they visit us, my mother goes on and on about how tired I look, how hard I obviously work, and how desperately I need to get some rest and make sure that I'm taking care of myself.

Meanwhile, as I sit on the couch soaking up all the sympathy and praise Mom can dish out, Meredith is busy breastfeeding a baby, refereeing a dispute over who gets the last yogurt tube, or scrubbing permanent marker off of a toddler's face. Lacking sleep, teetering on the edge of insanity, and already thinking about her evening glass of wine by ten in the morning, Meredith can't help but notice that my mother seems oblivious to her daughter-in-law's challenges while fretting over the welfare of her beloved son. With every "Kindred, you work so hard" and "Son, you need to get some rest" that rolls off my mother's tongue, I can sense my wife's eyes rolling backward and feel the heat of her burning glare frying a hole in the back of my head.

The praise from Mom is enjoyable, but it comes at a price. Every thirty seconds of sympathy from my mother equates to roughly five minutes of wifely venting once Meredith and I are alone. Frustrated, Meredith will proceed to remind me of how much *she's* doing, how tired *she* is, and how nice it would be if someone would occasionally give *her* a pat on the back. As a parade of valid points spills forth from my wife's mouth, I usually sit on the end of the bed and stare back in silence. Often, I listen. Sometimes, I just look at her while I think about how cool it would have been to be the fifth member of the rock band KISS. Either way, I've learned that the best thing I can do is to just let Meredith finish. Let her get it all out. I dare not speak. Any attempt to counter, correct, or comment on anything my wife is saying might be mistakenly interpreted as suggesting that I am more deserving of encouragement and sympathy than she is. Such a miscommunication could easily result in unwanted yelling and an actual physical attack.

Of course, conflict travels in both directions. It's never a one-way street. As I've alluded to, Meredith can tick Mom off too. Whereas Meredith unloads on me behind closed doors, Mom uses the ole silent treatment. She gets quiet. Her normally talkative and kind demeanor becomes cold and stern. Meredith can tell she's done something to make Mom mad—she just usually doesn't know what it is.

The Dreaded No-Man's Land

In what way does tension between new mommy and mother-in-law affect your caveman? As I mentioned, he's the one caught in the middle. He gets it from both sides. He's torn between trying to support and reassure the mother of his child and not hurting his own mother's feelings. It's a tough place to be. Most cavemen I know have a tendency to go one of two ways.

Either he'll wear himself out trying to keep the peace, or he'll simply withdraw emotionally, hoping to ride out the storm until his child's grandparents go home. Occasionally, if he's bold or simply fed up, a caveman will sit down with his wife and mother and try to work things out. But this is a difficult undertaking, often initially met with emotional reactions that make him second-guess his decision and remind him why God mercifully allowed man to discover alcohol.

Perhaps you're one of the fortunate few mommies who doesn't experience much conflict with your mother-in-law. If so, great! One less issue to worry about. But if you're like the many who do have such run-ins, know that your caveman is trying to figure out how to best navigate this rocky terrain. He's stuck in a no-man's land—a place he doesn't want to be and has no control over. In many cases, the two women he loves and who are at odds with one another won't directly address each other concerning their differences. (They should, but too often they won't.) Instead, they just let things build up. They allow themselves to grow angrier and more resentful until they finally explode. And when they do, who is most likely there to catch the brunt of their blast? You got it—the caveman.

Many new mommies may feel like their caveman doesn't do enough to support them or back them up when it comes to conflicts with their mothers-in-law. Sometimes, this may actually be the case. In most cases, however, your caveman isn't meaning to make you feel unsupported or like he values his mother's feelings above your own. He just has a different perspective. While a man should always put his wife first and not hesitate to support her if her wishes regarding the children are not being properly adhered to by a grandparent, he also remembers a time when he was a little boy and his mom was always there for him. Thus, it's understandable that he might want to exhaust all other possible solutions before having to say something that might hurt his mother's feelings.

Finally, because your caveman is already secure in your abilities as a mother, he also may not feel threatened or undermined by a grandparent's actions the way you do. What you see as an attempt to disregard your wishes or hijack your parental authority, your husband may simply view as a case of over-excited grandparents trying to love on and spoil their grandkid.

A United Front

That's not to say that your feelings aren't valid if you believe your caveman should do more to support you. They may very well be. You may be right. Just know that while you might feel frustrated, thinking he's not doing enough to back up your "mommy decisions," he's likely feeling frustrated because he can't figure out why everyone can't "just get along."

Once again, communication is the ultimate cure. Once you've gotten the chance to vent about how you feel, the two of you have to be able to talk and come up with some clear ground rules. In what areas are you prepared to be flexible and let grandparents do their own thing? In what areas will you not compromise and insist that grandparents respect your wishes without bending the rules? How will the two of you handle it if a grandparent has a less-than-ideal reaction to your decision to stand firm on certain issues?

Getting on the same page is essential to presenting a united front. Even with good communication, there may still be some tension. Your "united front" might initially hurt someone's feelings or leave a grandparent feeling offended. But at least the two of you will be unified and not at odds with one another.

In general, we cavemen recognize that you mommies are the leading authorities on your babies. We want to help and support you. We trust your judgment regarding the child's welfare the vast majority of the time. Just don't assume your caveman will know automatically where you want the lines drawn regarding rules for the baby if the two of you haven't talked. Unfortunately, we often don't intuitively pick up on what you're thinking. However, once the boundaries are clearly drawn and cavemen know what they are, most of them are prepared to back you up and make sure your wishes are respected and adhered to—even by your mother-in-law.

Chapter 13:
Married in Babyland

This book, first and foremost, is about a relationship. More specifically, it's about your relationship with your new or soon-to-be daddy. Why is nurturing this relationship so important? As a father of five kids, I can tell you without hesitation that the most important thing you can provide for your child is a strong, loving, secure relationship between Mommy and Daddy. Trust me, when exemplified by a sincere and selfless relationship in which both spouses truly appreciate, serve, and honor one another, the marriage bond creates a sense of permanency and security that your child or children long for and desperately need. If you have or are going to have kids, it's essential that you meet all the twists and turns of marriage with a deep conviction that your baby is counting on you and your spouse to be close.

Love Is a Decision

Sadly, in today's culture, divorce is considered every bit as normal as staying together. Keeping a marriage strong enough to last and grow in love and intimacy isn't easy. It takes a conviction that your commitment to one another is for life and that you meant all that "for better or worse, until death do us part" stuff you said on your wedding day. It takes devotion to one another, to the institution of marriage itself, and to your kids. And it takes resolve to say that, no matter what, you and your spouse will find a way to stay together and grow in your love for one another as time goes on. In other words, marriage takes character and a boatload of emotional strength.

A strong marriage also requires understanding that love is not a feeling or an emotion. Love isn't just goose bumps and butterflies every time your significant other walks into the room. Love that lasts a lifetime is far bigger than romance and being swept off your feet every time you look deeply into your loved one's eyes. Oh sure, your marriage should have its fair share of emotionally pleasing moments. There should be many times when you experience feelings of excitement, sexual attraction, and the desire to engage in playful flirting with one another. Of course you want your emotions to be onboard with your commitment to one another as a married couple. But emotions are just one aspect of love; they don't define it or even determine whether or not it's still there.

Love is ultimately a decision (or, should I say, a series of decisions). It's a decision to make your spouse's needs more important than your own. It's a decision to love your spouse the way God calls you to and the way God loves you, even when your spouse fails to love you the same way in return. It's a decision to focus on what you should and can be for your spouse rather than what your spouse should and could be for you. Love requires focusing on what you can control (your own decisions) rather than what you can't (your spouse's decisions), and then choosing to act in a manner consistent with the vows you made when you got married.

Remembering that I always possess the ability to *choose* to love is both empowering and scary. It's empowering in that I can live with the peace and security of knowing that I ultimately control whether or not I remain committed to my marriage. No force beyond my control can rip my love and commitment to my wife away from me. But it's also scary because, in most cases, I can't blame anyone else, not even my spouse, if I give up on my marriage.

Marriage, Meet Baby

In 2011, Meredith and I celebrated our fourteenth wedding anniversary. The years have certainly flown. In fourteen years of marriage, Meredith and I have lived in two states, five cities, and nine homes. We've seen our best-laid plans blow up in our faces, taken unexpected twists and turns, zigged when we should have zagged, and at times slipped temporarily into madness. We've lived through the pain and sorrow of three miscarriages, experienced the joys and blessings of having five beautiful children, built friendships with people that mean the world to us, and owned two dogs. Through highs, lows, career changes, family struggles, the death of old dreams, and the birth of new ones, Meredith and I have held on tight. We've laughed together, cried together, prayed together, and on many occasions fought rounds that made most pay-per-view boxing matches look like little-girl games of pat-a-cake. Still, here we are—well into our second decade together. After all this time, Meredith is still my best friend.

Even when my wife does things that leave me fuming inwardly and murmuring angry words under my breath, there's still no one else I want to be with. She's five-foot-four of sheer passion. (She'll try to tell you that she's five-four and a half, but don't believe her.) There's not a smile on earth that compares to hers, and when she walks in the room, every other woman still pales in comparison in my eyes. Yep, I'm a lucky man. I'm an aluminum ring set with a diamond. I'm a discount beer that somehow wound up on display next to fine champagne. Despite the tugs and pulls of parenthood, our marriage is even stronger now that we have kids.

But whether spouses are best friends or not, marriage changes once you have a baby. How can it not? You've taken what once was a relationship between two adults and thrown in an adorable, cuddly, screaming, poop-producing mini-person who can't be reasoned with and has no appreciation for the fact that you and your caveman need eight hours of sleep each night in order to function as competent human beings. You've gone from couple to family. It's an awesome and rewarding jump, but it's also a challenging and educational transition.

Any young or expecting mother reading this is probably not surprised by my "revelation" that babies impact marriages. What you might find interesting, however, is what men often are feeling and perceiving as these transformations take place.

Can We Talk?

Effective communication is not always easy, even before you become parents. Once a baby arrives, things get even more complicated. Sometimes, Daddy wants to communicate with Mommy, only to be frustrated that Mommy can't devote her total attention to him because she's preoccupied with a crying, nursing, or regurgitating child. Other times, Mommy needs to talk, only to discover Daddy is buried in work or zoned out in front of the television with only two functioning brain cells after helping to get the baby down for the night. No doubt about it, parenthood requires learning to work around some new obstacles to communication.

I've found that many guys are like I was when I became a dad. Most nights, following a tiring day of work, I just wanted to veg once the baby was asleep. I didn't want to talk about my day. I didn't want to answer a bunch of questions. I just wanted to sit and stare. Many nights, however, Meredith was different. Once the baby was asleep or at least quiet, she often wanted some adult conversation. She wanted to connect. I'd sit on the couch expecting to watch *Law & Order* or perhaps *Fox News*, only to be joined by my wife who wanted to tell me all about the great deal she'd found on diapers that day or wow me with stories of my daughter's most recent bowel movement.

Even more challenging was when Meredith started wanting my opinion about things I really hadn't thought about.

"What color highlights should I get in my hair?"

"What outfit should the baby wear tomorrow?"

"What do you think of my new shirt?"

"How many nursing bras do you think I should own?"

I didn't know. I just wanted to drink my Coke and watch Bill O'Reilly yell at a liberal for a few minutes.

I love my wife. I wanted to be supportive. But many evenings, I was so tired that it was all I could do just to look in her direction and muster a weak, "Uh, huh." I could see her. I noticed her mouth moving. But all I could hear was that distorted grown-up voice from the Charlie Brown cartoons. I wasn't trying to be rude. It was just that, after being up late the night before singing lullabies to my crying daughter, working all day at a job, and spending the evening helping with the baby once I got home, I was brain dead.

The fact is, most of us men don't understand why women have to talk about their day anyway. We could see it if something big happened. She won the lottery. She single-handedly stopped a bank robbery. She found Jimmy Hoffa's remains under the mound of used baby wipes and petrified Cheerios on the floor of our minivan. But as much as each of us loves our wife, most of us guys just can't find the fascination in hearing about everything she and her best friend discussed that day on the telephone.

That's not to say that women are the ones who've got it wrong. It's safe to say we guys don't talk enough. Surely we owe it to our better halves to listen more. We need to recognize that the mothers of our young children are often starving for adult contact. This is especially true if they are stay-at-home moms. Many new mothers spend most of their days cleaning spills, wiping tiny butts, nursing little boob suckers, and carrying on conversations that consist of phrases like, "Mommy's little cutie wutie..." and "Who's dat with a wittle stinky in his pants?"

We dads need to be more sensitive to your plight. Regardless of how tired we are at the end of a long day, it is important that we learn to take time to talk to our wives. We need to listen as you tell us about your day or express things that have been on your mind. We need to share with you about our day as well. (And, yes, we need to say a bit more than "It was fine.") Whether you are a mommy who works or predominantly stays at home, we fellas need to recognize your need to vent, connect, and, at times, live vicariously through a husband who spent the day in a world where people don't smell of diaper cream and baby formula.

Turning off the tube and tuning in to our wives at the end of a long day is often not cavemen's natural inclination. The good news is that any insensitivity or selfishness on our part usually isn't intended to communicate a lack of love. We're just beat and, perhaps, overwhelmed. For many men, having some time alone in silence or in front of the TV with nothing else to think about is how we decompress from the day's worries and recharge our batteries. While many stay-at-home mommies gain energy from some adult contact, men who work outside the home have spent the day getting their fill of adult contact. In fact, we're probably sick of adult contact. Heck, for a lot of guys, half the adults they "contacted" during the day, they didn't like anyway. In short, any arguments or hurt feelings that arise from differing expectations about communication often can be traced back to a clash of conflicting needs.

Having different needs is, of course, a poor excuse for men to be selfish or fail to pay some much needed attention to their wives. But my hope is that by sharing the reasons men are silent or seem "zoned out," I can perhaps reassure young mommies that their cavemen haven't lost interest in them. More than that, I want them to know that, with some tactful maneuvering on their part, there's some real hope for improving communication in Babyland.

Would You Like to Make an Appointment?

One suggestion I have that might help communication is to try setting appointments to talk. Pick a time that your caveman seems fairly attentive (i.e., not exhausted or in the middle of doing something he deems important). Then, talk to him about thinking ahead. Suggest that he plan on giving you a certain block of time at the end of each day, specifically set aside to give you his complete attention. He'll likely do best if you give him an actual time span: fifteen minutes, thirty minutes, or so on. Politely remind him that, once the demands of work and the duties of fatherhood have wound down for the day, there is still one more person who needs him. In fact, it's the most important person in his life—*YOU!*

A wife doesn't have to be shy about claiming her rightful place as the number-one person in her husband's life. As a new mommy, you *should* come before the job, the boss, the customers, and the need to relax. You should also come before the children. Don't feel selfish or apologize for it. You're strengthening your family. Not only are you building a stronger marriage, you're building more security for your kids as well. Nothing makes kids feel happier or safer than when they know Mommy and Daddy love each other more than anybody else in the world. So help your husband remember that you need some time each day too. Just know that your little "reminder" will go over much better if it is shared as part of a calm and loving conversation, rather than in the heat of an emotional argument or with the ring of an agitated tone.

Oh, and if you really want to set yourself up to win, make sure you present your requests from the angle of wanting to connect with your caveman because you love him, need him, and value talking to him. Make him feel that you want to connect with him daily not just because you need to be heard, but also because you respect him and think he's awesome. A guy thrives on feeling respected and admired by the woman he loves.

But what if the time you set aside to talk arrives and your caveman still seems beat and inattentive? Rather than getting mad (which will likely only produce conflict), try asking him if he needs some time to unwind. When he says "yes" (or grunts affirmatively), then ask if you can talk to him in twenty minutes. He will likely appreciate the fact that you considered his need and will usually agree. That way, he gets the time he needs to prepare to listen and talk. Simultaneously, you avoid the frustration of wondering when you'll ever get the chance to connect. He might still be in his cave, but at least you know when he'll be emerging to have a conversation.

Caveman versus Baby

As dumb as it sounds, we young fathers sometimes can't help but feel a little bit jealous of a new baby. Yes, I know it seems ridiculous. It's a baby, for cryin' out loud! A baby needs constant attention, especially from Mommy. Certainly, a rational adult male should understand and be cool with that. After all, it's his baby too. Don't we fathers love our kids? Don't we want all their physical and emotional needs to be met? Why don't we dads just get a grip? Why don't we pick on somebody our own size? C'mon! How self-centered can someone get?

All I can say is, don't forget what gender you're dealing with. That's not a shot at us guys. Both men and women can be selfish. But men are the ones who sometimes resent the fact that the baby garners the majority of their spouses' time and energy. We're the ones who can feel a little hurt and pushed to the back burner once our wives become mothers. I think it can help moms if, rather than simply getting disgusted with dejected cavemen, they can understand a little bit of what might be going through their husbands' prehistoric minds to make them feel this way.

More than his pride lets him show, a man longs for attention and a sense of admiration from his wife. He bases much of his security on feeling like the woman he loves most thinks he's awesome. Your caveman savors the notion that, no matter what kind of a beating he took at work that day or how badly he was tempted to feel like a failure, there's still one person who thinks he's the greatest thing on earth—*YOU*! Thus, when the baby comes and saps all your attention, it's not just that he feels like he's being ignored; it's deeper than that. He feels like he's losing his biggest fan. The woman who used to be so in tune with his demeanor that she could pick up on his insecurities and effectively counter them to build him back up is now so tired or busy with the baby that she often doesn't have the time or energy to notice when he's needing to feel like she still loves, respects, and admires him. And it affects him—deeply.

More than anything, your husband wants to feel respected in your eyes. If he seems distant, withdrawn, or possibly a little frustrated by the fact that the baby gets most of your time and energy, take a few moments to tell him something you respect about him. Write him a note informing him how much you recognize all his hard work and admire him for his desire to take care of you and the baby. I'm telling ya, it works wonders, and it doesn't take long.

Hey, I'm not saying it's right for men to feel competitive with a baby for mommy's attention. In fact, you can make a darned good argument that it's selfish and immature. I'm just saying that it's not uncommon for guys to experience these emotions once a new baby arrives. How you choose to use this information is totally up to you.

Sulk, Mope, and Mumble

Of course, women can feel neglected or like their needs are being ignored too. The difference is that women tend to do a much better job of verbally expressing themselves. Even if a woman initially responds with an irritated silence, she'll usually only give her caveman a limited amount of time to figure out on his own that he's offended her before she finally can't take it anymore and has to say something. Men often don't say a word, at least not without some serious prompting.

The culprit is our pride. Take, for instance, feeling jealous of the baby. We know that we *shouldn't* feel competitive with our infant son or daughter. We know how selfish and ridiculous such emotions are. We recognize that only a real jerk would insist on some attention from a new mommy who is exhausted and rightfully pouring out her time and attention to care for a baby. Our heads get it. The problem is that our hearts and egos don't. Therefore, though we tell ourselves we shouldn't—and try to convince ourselves we don't—we sometimes still feel hurt, jealous, and neglected.

So what do men do when they're feeling hurt and neglected but don't want to admit it? We do what we've done for centuries: sulk, mope, and mumble. We men are great sulkers, mopers, and mumblers. Sulking, moping, and mumbling are effective ways for men to complain while still convincing ourselves that we're not really complaining. Sulking, moping, and mumbling communicate to our wives that we're not happy. They allow us to act surprised when you women ask us if something is bothering us, even though we really wanted you to pick up on the fact that, well, *something is bothering us*. Part of us doesn't want to admit that we're feeling ignored and unloved. That part doesn't want to talk. The other part of us would love to tell you what we need. That part wants to 'fess up. Sulking, moping, and mumbling are effective caveman methods for getting women to "make" us talk, while allowing us to cling to the notion that we didn't really want or need to. It allows us to tell ourselves that we only opened up about what's eating at us because the new mommies in our lives asked.

Sorry ladies, I can't give you a magic formula to ensure that your cavemen will never sulk, mope, or mumble again. All I can offer is the insight that, in a strangely selfish way, they may be doing it because they love and, believe it or not, miss you.

The Outer Limits

While I can't offer a fail-proof method to ensure that your caveman never gets emotional, I can offer one practical piece of advice: *talk*. Sit down and have an open and honest discussion about what the first eighteen to twenty-four months of parenthood is going to look like. If you already have some kiddos, then you pretty much know what to expect and your husband may be less likely to get his feelings hurt. (Plus, he'll be busy taking care of the older kids.)

During the first two years of a child's life, it's essential that Mom and Dad revolve their lives around the baby. Heck, it's necessary just to keep the little bambino alive. Babies can't talk, can't walk, can't clean themselves, can't feed themselves, and certainly can't be reasoned with. When a baby poops or cries, you gotta respond.

In most families (though not in all), Mom tends to be the primary caregiver during this period. Dad should be right there helping too, but he's more like the teaching assistant. Mommy is the professor with the PhD in infantology. Thus, as baby squirms, crawls, cries, pees, poops, and burps at the center of the household universe, Mommy is usually the closest celestial body rotating around the tiny newcomer, tending to his or her every need. Daddy rotates too. But he orbits along the outer limits. His job is to stay in sync with Mommy and be prepared to take over whenever the professor needs a break or some backup. (Dad will rotate much closer, of course, if Mommy works a full-time job and/or Daddy is a stay-at-home father.)

My point is that, in most cases, it is Mommy who will need to focus most of her attention on the child during the first two years of parenthood. Daddy will just have to accept it. That's just the way it must be. Discussing this reality ahead of time so that Dad knows what's coming often helps prevent some of the dejected feelings a father might otherwise feel. Talking to other couples also can prove beneficial. It gives your caveman the chance to learn from other dads that what he's feeling and experiencing is pretty normal. By helping your caveman understand and accept the new dynamic in your baby-makes-three world, you can help facilitate an easier transition.

A Temporary Layover

You can also encourage your caveman with the fact that the baby-centered universe I just described will only exist until the child is about two years old (give or take). After all, the parent-child relationship is NOT the predominant relationship in the family. Nope, that title belongs to the marriage. Communicate to your caveman that you understand the child-centeredness that accompanies the infant years is a temporary layover. By doing this, you reassure your caveman that he won't play second fiddle to the child for long. Informing him that you realize the marriage has to return to the center of the household solar system sometime during your child's second year of life, encourages him with some much-needed light at the end of the Babyland tunnel. As a result, your caveman will have an easier time fending off the occasional temptations to feel neglected or forgotten by reminding himself *This is just the way it's going to have to be for a while—BUT IT WON'T BE THIS WAY FOREVER.*

Of course, marriage will never be the way it was before you had kids. You will forever be parents. There will be times well beyond your children's first two years of life when they will require loving attention. There will be dates you can't go on because of a sick child or a babysitter that had to cancel. Many nights, your quality time together will have to wait until the children are in bed or at least not under foot. You inevitably will have more than one conversation or quiet moment interrupted by the screams of a child who has skinned a knee and believes that he or she requires a band aid right away in order to save his or her leg from amputation. No big deal. That's parenthood. Just never forget that nurturing and maintaining a great marriage is a parent's number one job!

Chapter 14:
Birds and Bees in Babyland

Let's talk about sex, shall we? Heck, we might as well finish on a fun note. Plus, let's be honest; sex is a huge part of the marriage relationship. You and your caveman have had it at least once or you wouldn't be reading a book for new and expecting mommies. Given the importance of the sexual relationship between a husband and wife, I feel it would be irresponsible of me not to address it.

Before I go further, there are a few points I would like to make clear. First, know that everything I have to say about sex is intended to be taken within the context of marriage. While I might have fun with the topic, never forget that everything I say is in reference to the physical relationship between a husband and wife.

Second, while I deeply respect the sexual relationship between men and women and certainly never want to say anything inappropriate, crude, or offensive, I also believe that God made sex to be thrilling. It bothers me that we married folks have let the unmarried world hijack all the fun when it comes to sex. The media and our culture paint a picture of unmarried sex as being exciting, passionate, and adventurous, while portraying married sex as being only slightly more interesting than curling highlights from the last winter Olympics. I strongly disagree with such suggestions! Married sex is awesome! It's much more meaningful and edifying than the unmarried counterfeit, and, unlike unmarried sex, actually produces greater security rather than insecurity in a relationship. In my opinion, married sex should be exciting, fun, and, if both spouses are up for it, creative and experimental.

Third, I want to reiterate that it is not my intention to offend any of my readers. That's one reason why I saved this chapter for last. If you aren't comfortable reading a chapter on sex that also has some fun with the topic for fear of being offended, then now's the time to stop reading this chapter. You can go ahead and skip to the closing of this book. Perhaps your reservations stem from your personal religious convictions. While I can't speak for all faiths, I can speak from a Christian perspective. If, like me, you are a Christian, know that there is nothing—*absolutely nothing*—in the Bible that suggests we marrieds shouldn't have every bit as much fun with sex as the rest of the world. It only tells us to reserve the good times for our marriage relationship.

Surface-to-Air Missiles

This just in: men like sex! We want to have sex with our wives. Even the times when a man feels "too tired" or "not in the mood" his mind can usually be changed rather quickly with a touch of his wife's hand or one look at her in the negligée she hasn't worn since last Valentine's Day. With most men, hormones almost always trump fatigue or emotions. We can be in the midst of a heated argument with our wives one minute and still be ready to have sex with them the next. If we haven't talked to our spouse all day, it doesn't hinder us from still being ready to have sex with her when we get home. We don't need a certain mood or time to emotionally engage. We're like surface-to-air missiles: just put off a little heat and we're ready to launch.

Women, of course, are generally different. They're much more difficult to figure out. (At least men think they are.) Circumstances—such as wanting to have a baby or becoming a new mommy—can greatly impact a woman's desire for sex. Just when a man thinks he's got the rules of the sexual game figured out, his wife's desire to conceive, the news that she's pregnant, or the arrival of a baby changes things again. It's enough to make some guys wish they had joined the priesthood.

From Connecting to Conception

It's very interesting how the sexual dynamic in a household changes once the woman decides she wants a baby. Correct me if I'm wrong, but don't women usually link sex to the depth of a relationship? Don't you have to be in the mood? Don't you normally need plenty of foreplay? Whereas most men are like a microwave (just punch the buttons and it's ready in seconds), aren't women more like a conventional oven, requiring men to turn the knob to the right setting so things can heat up? As a somewhat typical guy, my idea of foreplay rarely consists of more than an affirmative answer to the question, "Want to?" My wife's, however, usually involves a drawn-out and often complicated ritual that requires conversation, sensitivity, attention, and affection—much of which must occur hours, if not days, before we actually have sex. And it all falls under the category of what women call *connecting*.

What exactly is "connecting"? If your caveman is like most, he's probably not totally sure. For me, connecting with my wife is a lot like trigonometry was in high school: I occasionally get the right answer, but I can't really tell you how I did it. Sometimes, I'll buy a bottle of wine, rub my wife's shoulders, and use every compliment in the book to try to sweep Meredith off her feet, only to find myself alone at one o'clock in the morning watching a Chuck Norris infomercial. At other times, I'll be cleaning a dirty dish or picking up after the kids, suddenly to notice Meredith eyeing me with a "drop that half-eaten pop tart you just found under the couch and make mad, passionate love to me now" look. No doubt about it, connecting is complex for us guys. All we know for sure is that we have to figure it out if we ever want to have sex.

The Mathematics of Connecting

To make the normal sexual dynamic even harder, men find that women often get very frustrated with us for not being better at connecting. If connecting is a math equation, then we guys are the dumbfounded math students sitting in class and trying desperately to figure out how the heck X equals 27. Women, on the other hand, are the insanely smart professors who can't understand why we don't get it. Just like that foreign-born calculus instructor you had in college who got frustrated every time you couldn't grasp "simple" math concepts, women think men are either stupid or deliberately insensitive for not knowing how to connect. Meanwhile, we guys are pulling out our hair and thinking, "Forget learning to add fractions, just give me the cotton-pickin' answer!"

Men just want a list. Tell us what to do and we'll do it. Tell us what it takes to connect and we'll connect till the cows come home. But the cruel irony is that the more we ask you women how to connect, the more we contribute to the lack of connecting. The way you figure it, if we loved you, we'd already know how to connect. Therefore, any requested assistance only frustrates you further and solidifies your perception of us as selfish and insensitive.

From a man's perspective, it's not a logical process. In fact, it's downright maddening. It's like a game. Connect and we get sex. But we have to figure out how to connect on our own because asking a woman for hints automatically places us further away from connecting. It's like playing an adult version of Chutes and Ladders. One minute, the game seems to be going well. We're climbing ladders and thinking about the physical pleasure awaiting us just beyond the top rung. Then, before we know what's happened, we land on the wrong square and *swoosh*, down we go! No sex for us. It's very frustrating.

Sex Goes Wireless

But let's return to my original point: sex changes once a woman wants a baby. Connection is no longer essential. Sex goes wireless. Now it's you women who are initiating. Now you're the ones up for a "quickie" before work or in between episodes of your favorite TV shows. And it's all because you want to get pregnant.

At first, most cavemen love it! "Finally" we cheer, "sex the way it must have been in the Garden of Eden!" No complicated games. No mystery path to connection. Just simple, instinctual, carnal love-making! "So what if it's just because she wants a baby," we tell ourselves. We could care less about the motives: *we get to have sex without the math!*

Once the initial bliss wears off, however, men tend to find conception sex a little awkward and, at times, deflating. After a while, many cavemen even think it begins to feel like work. To most men, the idea of sex seeming like a chore is an alien concept, but not to men whose wives have craved a baby. A woman with baby fever can turn a home into a totalitarian state. For men, it's like living under a tyrannical war lord. They're expected to be at their wives' beck and call, subject to their every sexual command. The phrase "I'm ovulating" becomes synonymous with "Drop your pants NOW, you dog!" Sure it's fun sometimes. But man, how often can one five-foot-four living organism ovulate? And why do women always seem to ovulate when the game is on, after their husbands have just gotten home from a hard day at work, or when their cavemen are trying to sleep?

As for when we were trying to conceive, even when I was in the mood, Meredith restricted us to only certain positions. Apparently, certain sexual positions are better for making babies than others. I guess sperm just won't swim if they dive in from the wrong end of the pool. At first I didn't mind—sex is sex. But after a while I wanted some variety. Heck, even Mr. Rogers changed his sweater once in a while.

The Weather Channel

A woman on a baby hunt can also turn your home into a research center. Sex becomes a science. A wannabe mom somehow knows what days and hours she should have sex, when her caveman's sperm count will likely be the highest, and when her egg should be in its ready position. For us wannabe dads, it's almost overwhelming. We're constantly inundated with facts, conception-related data, calculated predictions, and, in some cases, charts and visual images. It's like living in a sexual version of *The Weather Channel*. Most of the time, we half expect our wannabe mom to whip out a map with satellite images and burst into a baby-making forecast:

"As you can see from this reproductive cloud forming over my uterus, there's a strong ovulation front moving in from the north. This means that we should expect a sperm shower sometime between 11 a.m. and 1 p.m. tomorrow, presenting a likely chance of conception, followed by periods of cooler temperatures in the bedroom in the weeks to come."

I remember when my wife and I were trying to have our first baby. Meredith had ovulation kits, books, charts, and every other product on the market that was supposed to help a woman conceive. She even dictated to me what underwear I could wear. As far as sperm are concerned, jockey shorts are apparently the kiss of death. I had to wear boxers. Boxers are cool for some guys, but I just couldn't get used to them. Every time I stopped walking, my little amigos kept trying to go an extra step. Whenever I went for a run or played a game of basketball, I thought someone had dropped a bag of marbles down my shorts. I felt like a sentence with dangling participles.

A Rough Ride in Coach

Eventually, the wireless, weather-channel sex worked. Meredith did get pregnant. But one thing remains certain: conception sex was quite an experience—very different from the normal sexual dynamic that Meredith and I had grown accustomed to in our pre-baby-making world.

For men, especially, the changes from connection sex to conception sex and back to connection sex can be quite a ride. After all, we guys don't know when all the twists and turns are coming. We're not the ones flying the plane. While you women are the pilots, securely buckled in the cockpit and aware of the impending weather conditions, we men are the unprepared coach passengers getting the heck beat out of us every time you dip and dive through pockets of sexual turbulence. Just when we think we understand connecting and can safely stow our bags in an overhead bin, your desire to have a baby leads to sex unplugged and an immediate need to fasten our seatbelts. Then, once we've gotten use to sex on demand and being free to walk about the cabin, a little blue line appears on a home pregnancy test and we're suddenly knocked off our feet by a rapid drop in conjugal altitude.

My point is simply this: cavemen can feel confused by, and left out of, all the changes and decisions surrounding pregnancy sex. Never forget, we're still trying to figure out the whole connecting thing. Don't assume it's an easy adjustment for your caveman. Sure, he'll likely love the high demand for sex at first, but after a while his ego may take a hit. As funny as it sounds, he might start to feel like he's only there to make a baby. And make no mistake, regardless of what your caveman tries to tell you, he does want to feel like you want *him*, not just a child. So you might want to stroke his ego some. Make him feel like you're enjoying yourself, not just tracking your eggs on radar. Just like you need him to say and do things that reassure you that you're sexually attractive during pregnancy, he needs to feel sexually desirable too—even though he may never admit it.

Also, you and your caveman need to work to maintain a strong sexual relationship even after you've conceived. You both still have sexual needs after you're pregnant. Sure the sexual pace may drop off some. That's understandable. After all, your body will be going through massive hormonal changes. Just make sure you give your caveman the occasional "heads up" to let him know what you're thinking and what you feel realistic sexual expectations are. Tell him why your desire for sex is different. Don't just assume he understands. He'll appreciate some explanation—even more than he realizes. After all, you can't let a caveman hunt all the time while you're trying to conceive then suddenly take his club away once you know you're having a baby. If you do, you're likely to find him moping in the corner of the cave and wondering why, after weeks in the Garden of Eden, he's now got to go back to calculus class.

Sex on a Timer

Fast forward to Babyland. One of the biggest areas affected by parenthood is sex. Before children, sex is an event. There's romance. Often, there's a date. Usually, both participants have showered at some point in the previous twenty-four hours. You take your time. You connect (that is if your caveman can figure out how to). The house is all yours. If the headboard's hitting the wall, who cares? It just means you're having a good night. If one of you feels inclined to make loud animal noises, you go for it. If you want to don a loin cloth and play a round of Tarzan meets Jane, so what—it's fun. You enjoy the experience. There are no boundaries. When it's over, if you want to walk to the fridge and sit on the couch buck naked to eat a sandwich and watch television, you do it (hopefully remembering to wipe down the couch afterwards, especially if you have leather furniture).

With kids, the rules change drastically. Now sex is on a timer. Now a wife says things like, "If we're gonna do it, we gotta do it now; the baby will wake up soon." You used to call out your caveman's name during sex; now you call out the number of minutes he has left before you have to get up and tend to a crying infant. Sexy lingerie gives way to flannel pajama pants and t-shirts that smell of spit-up. Banging headboards and animal calls are muffled by sounds of "Shhhhh! You'll wake the baby!" Even the art of emotionally connecting is cast aside as a young mommy insists that her caveman hurry up and finish so that she can get some sleep before the next round of breastfeeding begins. For a guy, it's like playing a game of Double-Dutch jump rope; he has to jump in at just the right time, or he's likely to miss his turn.

The male ego usually takes a beating in this post-baby-sex world. Many cavemen have a difficult time not getting their feelings hurt when their once welcomed sexual advances are repeatedly rebuffed with statements like, "Not now, my nipples hurt." Even when new moms do muster the willingness for sex, your cavemen don't always get the fact that the idea of a nap is far more likely to elicit an orgasm than any sexual maneuver they might perform. Few things burst a man's love-making bubble faster than the realization that his wife's moaning is actually due to the fact that it's just dawned on her she forgot to buy diapers at the store. But hey, that's the sexual reality when you have a baby. Unfortunately, for many guys (especially first-time dads), it's tough not to take it personal.

The Magic Kingdom Is Closed

It's even harder on guys when you consider the cruelest sexual irony of all: new-mommy breasts! New moms have enormous breasts. Guess what: most men really like enormous breasts (on women, that is). But the horrible part for new daddies is the fact that new-mommy breasts aren't for them. No, that pleasure has been reserved for a football-sized parasite who has zero appreciation for what he's been given access to and feels no guilt about monopolizing all the fun. Meanwhile, all Daddy can do is sit off to the side like a dejected child, trying to look understanding as he inwardly cries, "Can I play too?"

It's one of nature's meanest jokes. For a husband, it's like finally getting that big raise, only to learn that Congress has changed the tax laws and the IRS is taking all the money. It's like watching someone else enjoy a day at Disney World while you have to wait in the parking lot. Then, when it's finally your turn, you run to the entrance of the Magic Kingdom, only to find that Snow White is tired after being with a dwarf all day and Fantasy Land has closed.

Without a doubt, we guys need to learn to suck it up more and not get offended. But, the truth is, we still want to feel that our wives find us desirable. We want to think that they at least *want* to have sex with us. Therefore, anything a new mommy can do to help her caveman feel like he's still got it (even if she's too tired to want it right now) goes a long way.

Audibles

If your caveman is a sports fan, you may want to use this helpful football analogy to help him understand what he needs to do to nurture a healthy sex life in Babyland. When a quarterback wants to score a touchdown, he doesn't give up just because a few passes fall incomplete. No, he surveys the playing field, notes changes in the defense, and calls an *audible*. Simply stated, he changes the play he was going to run to one that he thinks will work better against the defense he sees in front of him. In the same way, once baby arrives, the playbook has gotta change. The same old sexual game plan just won't get you there. A caveman has got to call audibles.

For instance, a caveman may need some coaching to understand that romantic dinners, while still nice from time to time, often aren't practical. Such approaches can no longer be a man's primary weapon for sweeping a woman with a baby off her feet and putting her in the mood. The definition of "foreplay" has changed a bit. Help your caveman realize that if he'll do some laundry, cook a meal, change some diapers, or just take the baby for a few hours so Mommy can get some rest, he's much more likely to score than if he brings home some flowers and a box of candy. Let him know that you may not throw yourself at him immediately (you'll probably want to get some sleep first). But, eventually, if done consistently and with sincerity, such gestures are going to pay some romantic dividends. One minute he'll be wiping baby lotion off his hands or making goo-goo, ga-ga sounds, and the next he'll be returning to your bedroom to find that Disney World is open and he gets to ride Space Mountain. It might take some trial and error, but, with your help, your caveman will figure it out. There are still touchdowns to be scored. He just has to change the plays.

Parting Grunts from an Average Caveman

As parents, most of us long to provide the best possible life for our kids. Too often, however, we can make the mistake of erroneously defining what it means to provide. If we caveman aren't careful, we'll fall into the trap of thinking that meeting our kids' needs predominantly means raising them in a beautiful suburban neighborhood, buying them nice clothes, bestowing on them all the material blessings you never had growing up, saving for their future, and perhaps sending them to a private school. While these things are certainly nice and, in some cases, can even give our kids a leg up in life, many parents end up missing the point. The pursuit of such "blessings" often demands so much time or creates so much stress for moms and dads that, if we're not careful as parents, we can actually sacrifice what's most important for our children in the name of "providing" for them.

Parents who are a little wiser understand that, while material provisions are great and to some degree necessary, they turn out to mean very little if we fail to provide loving leadership and guidance for our kids. Material blessings, if not accompanied by meaningful relationships with our children, turn out to be empty and even alienating in the end. Smart parents realize that what's most important is to invest emotionally in their kids. This doesn't mean we should build kid-centric homes in which all our time and attention go into the children, with nothing left over for our spouses, friends, careers, interests, and so on. But emotionally investing in our kids does mean that we spend time with them, get to know them, and, as they grow, make sure that they feel like Mom and Dad listen, care, and are aware of their personal passions and dreams.

Your Child's Greatest Need

Even the most well-intentioned and engaged parents can easily forget their child's greatest need. Of all the things you can give your child—material, emotional, or otherwise—I believe that the greatest (outside of nurturing their relationship with God) is to provide him or her with a home in which Mommy and Daddy deeply love each other. Nothing—ABSOLUTELY NOTHING— makes a child happier and more secure than having a mother and father who are constantly telling one another "I love you," kissing one another, hugging one another, expressing appreciation for one another, and showing that they respect and value one another. In short, the greatest gift you can give your child is a strong, loving, lifelong, committed relationship between you and your caveman.

This is largely why I've written this book. Yes, I wanted to have some fun and make you laugh. I hope you've gotten a chuckle or two as you've read my personal stories and my take on parenthood from a guy's perspective. But I mainly wanted to write this book because I believe you and your caveman are in a great position in life. As new or expecting parents, you have a golden opportunity. You have the chance to recognize the importance of nurturing and continuing to build a strong marriage while your kids are still young. Right off the bat, you get to benefit from the realization that your marriage relationship is the most crucial part of your parenting. By giving you new moms the inside scoop on us dads, I hope I have done a bit more than just enable you to laugh at my gender's expense. I'd like to think that I've provided a few helpful "Aha" moments. I hope you found one or two principles or tidbits of advice that you can use to better understand *your* caveman, thereby helping your communication and, in turn, your relationship.

Since, by necessity, I have had to address topics generally, there have no doubt been portions you've read that don't apply to your particular situation. But I hope there was a chapter or two, or perhaps a few subsections, which you found helpful and from which you gleaned some useful information.

Communication Instead of Killing

At the end of the day, this book is largely about communication. As I've mentioned, you can't read your caveman's mind (and, boy, is he glad you can't). He can't read yours (even though you often want him to). So talk. Sure, you'll need to be strategic sometimes. Tact goes a long way. There are better times than others to bring up certain topics. You or your caveman might blow it a few times by hitting the wrong nerve at the wrong time. Sometimes it takes trial and error. Don't let the fear of an argument or even a few failed attempts to have a constructive, open conversation stop you. In my experience, most problems in a relationship can be solved (or at least greatly alleviated) if couples will talk to each other AND to other couples they know and trust. Communication is key to a lasting relationship. That means it's key to your parenting too. Understand that your number one job as a parent is to protect your relationship with your spouse. Fail in this area and, trust me, nothing else you provide for your children will ever totally make up for it.

So there you go. Hopefully, you can trust that most men aren't trying to be insensitive Neanderthals who intentionally tick you off. Unfortunately, we're just naturally good at it. Like a fledgling eagle that learns to fly by instinct or whale calf that knows how to swim right out of its mother's womb, we men are genetically tailored to frustrate and baffle women—especially the women we love most in the world. Perhaps by understanding a little more about what makes daddies tick, you moms will find the will and the patience to bear with us and meet us at the door of our cave. I hope this book has proved useful to that end. If nothing else, maybe it's saved the life of a caveman or two. As a caveman myself, I never set out writing this book to justify men's behavior. Rather, my goal has simply been to shed light on the male way of thinking and why cavemen do the things they do. In the end, my only hope is that new and expecting mommies might read this, take pity on their cavemen, and, after considering all the options, decide not to kill them.

About the Author

Kindred Howard grew up in Asheboro, North Carolina, where he graduated from high school in 1987. In 1991, he completed his undergraduate at the University of North Carolina at Chapel Hill. After working for two years as a probation and parole officer in Charlotte, Kindred entered the full-time ministry in 1994 and later attended graduate school at Asbury Theological Seminary and Georgia State University.

After roughly eleven years serving nondenominational churches in Charlotte and Atlanta, Kindred resigned from the ministry in 2005. Following a brief stint teaching and working in sales, Kindred became the social studies coordinator for American Book Company, where he became the published author or co-author of over twenty educational books currently used by public schools in eight states.

In 2008, Kindred left American Book Company to start his own freelance writing business: KB Howard Freelance Writing Services. Two years later, in 2010, Kindred founded Family Upward: Marriage, Parent, & Family Life Coaching, an organization for which he currently serves as president.

Today, Kindred is a professional marriage and parenting coach who works closely with engaged couples, spouses, and parents to help them deal effectively with issues that have impact on their relationships. Kindred is also an award-winning writer and an acclaimed public speaker who writes and regularly addresses audiences about the topics of marriage and family.

Kindred met his wife, Meredith, in 1996, and the two were married less than eighteen months later. After enduring the sorrow and disappointment of three miscarriages, Kindred and Meredith were blessed with the arrival of their first child, their daughter Emerson, in 2003. Their two oldest sons, William and Carson, followed in 2005 and 2007. In 2010, Kindred and Meredith fulfilled their longtime dream to adopt when they became the proud parents of their two youngest sons, Samuel and Asher (twin boys born in Ethiopia).

About Family Upward

Family Upward: Marriage, Parent, & Family Life Coaching is an organization devoted to empowering engaged couples, married couples, and parents with the tools they need to build stronger marriages and raise happy, secure, and well-disciplined kids. Founded by Kindred Howard in 2010, Family Upward uses Biblically-based, common-sense approaches to positively resolve marriage and parenting-related issues. The principles and practicals that Family Upward coaches teach have consistently proven effective to help families strengthen and maintain their most precious relationships.

Family Upward's founder, Kindred Howard, is a protégé of nationally renowned parenting expert John Rosemond and works in close conjunction with the Rosemond Leadership Parenting Institute. Feel free to contact Kindred directly about scheduling a coaching session or perhaps a public speaking engagement or seminar at your church, PTA, HOA clubhouse, place of business, or other organization.

www.familyupward.com

kindred@familyupward.com